American Language Hub

LEVEL 4B
Student's Book

LOUIS ROGERS

macmillan education

Contents

Irregular Verbs

Base form	Simple past	Past participle
be	was/were	been
become	became	become
begin	began	begun
break	broke	broken
bring	brought	brought
build	built	built
buy	bought	bought
can	could	(been able to)
catch	caught	caught
choose	chose	chosen
come	came	come
cost	cost	cost
cut	cut	cut
do	did	done
drink	drank	drunk
eat	ate	eaten
fall	fell	fallen
feel	felt	felt
find	found	found
forget	forgot	forgotten
get	got	got
give	gave	given
go	went	gone/been
grow	grew	grown
have	had	had
hear	heard	heard
hit	hit	hit
hold	held	held
hurt	hurt	hurt
keep	kept	kept
know	knew	known
leave	left	left
lend	lent	lent

Base form	Simple past	Past participle
let	let	let
lose	lost	lost
make	made	made
mean	meant	meant
meet	met	met
must	had to	(had to)
pay	paid	paid
put	put	put
read	read	read
ride	rode	ridden
run	ran	run
say	said	said
see	saw	seen
sell	sold	sold
set	set	set
shut	shut	shut
sing	sang	sung
sit	sat	sat
sleep	slept	slept
speak	spoke	spoken
spell	spelled	spelled
spend	spent	spent
stand	stood	stood
steal	stole	stolen
take	took	taken
teach	taught	taught
tell	told	told
think	thought	thought
throw	threw	thrown
understand	understood	understood
wear	wore	worn
win	won	won
write	wrote	written

PHONETIC SYMBOLS											
Single vowels			Diphthongs			Consonants					
/ɪ/	fish	/fɪʃ/	/uw/	new	/nuw/	/p/	pen	/pen/	/s/	snake	/sneɪk/
/iː/	bean	/biːn/	/eɪ/	face	/feɪs/	/b/	bag	/bæg/	/z/	zoo	/zuː/
/ʊ/	foot	/fʊt/	/ɔɪ/	boy	/bɔɪ/	/t/	tea	/tiː/	/ʃ/	shop	/ʃɒp/
/uː/	shoe	/ʃuː/	/oʊ/	nose	/noʊz/	/d/	dog	/dɒg/	/ʒ/	television	/'telɪvɪʒən/
/e/	egg	/eg/	/ju/	use	/juz/	/ʧ/	chip	/ʧɪp/	/m/	map	/mæp/
/ə/	mother	/'mʌðər/	/aɪ/	eye	/aɪ/	/ʤ/	jazz	/ʤæz/	/n/	name	/neɪm/
/ɜː/	word	/wɜːrd/	/aʊ/	mouth	/maʊθ/	/k/	cake	/keɪk/	/ŋ/	ring	/rɪŋ/
/ɔː/	talk	/tɔːk/				/g/	girl	/gɜːrl/	/h/	house	/haʊs/
/æ/	back	/bæk/				/f/	film	/fɪlm/	/l/	leg	/leg/
/ʌ/	bus	/bʌs/				/v/	verb	/vɜːrb/	/r/	road	/roʊd/
/ɑː/	arm	/ɑːrm/				/θ/	thing	/θɪŋ/	/w/	want	/wɒnt/
/ɒ/	top	/tɒp/				/ð/	these	/ðiːz/	/j/	yes	/jes/

6 COMING OF AGE

It's widely believed that our ability to learn new things declines with age.

> Anyone who stops learning is old, whether at 20 or 80. Anyone who keeps learning stays young.
>
> Henry Ford

OBJECTIVES

- discuss rules in education
- talk about changes to education in your country
- discuss age milestones in your country
- debate the best time to start college
- give your opinion on an aspect of education
- write a report

Work with a partner. Discuss the questions.

1 Read the quote. Do you agree with Ford? Why/Why not?

2 What are the most important birthdays in your country (e.g. 18, 21, 50, etc)? How are they celebrated?

3 If you could give your younger self one piece of advice, what would it be and why?

6.1 The right method?

- Discuss rules in education
- Talk about changes to education in your country

G – **obligation, prohibition and permission**
V – **education**
P – **intonation to show interest**
S – **pronoun referencing**

LISTENING

A SPEAK Work in groups. Look at the school rules (1–6). Which do you think are reasonable? Which do you think are unreasonable? Why?

6.1 **B LISTEN FOR GIST** Listen to a radio interview about different school systems. Choose the best summary (1–3).

1. Both guests had a similar school experience but disagree about which system to use today.
2. Both guests enjoyed their school experience but disagree about the best system to use today.
3. Both guests agree that students need rules, and that current systems should be stricter.

6.1 **C LISTEN FOR DETAIL** Listen again. Complete the sentences with no more than two words from the interview.

1. In Jessica's school, students and teachers could ________________ on the rules.
2. Jessica thinks students behave better when they have the ________________ to make decisions.
3. Jessica thinks teenagers want more ________________ of their environment as they're becoming adults.
4. In Jessica's school, students got excellent ______________ ________________ and went on to further education and to have good jobs.
5. In Andrew's school, everyone had to have the ________________ hair, bags and clothes.
6. Children who broke the rules in Andrew's school had to wear ________________ around their necks.
7. Andrew thinks more ________________ make things fairer because all teachers behave the same.
8. Jessica felt her experience at school made her more ________________ when she left.

D SPEAK Work in pairs. Which school would you prefer to study at? Why?

SCHOOL RULES

1. Bathroom breaks during class limited to three times a week.
2. Students must not dye their hair.
3. Any student arriving more than five minutes late will be given cleaning duties.
4. Male students are strictly forbidden from having facial hair.
5. Shorts may not be worn between September 15th and May 15th.
6. No groups larger than five anywhere on school grounds.

GRAMMAR

Obligation, prohibition and permission

6.2 **A Complete the extracts with the words in the box. Then listen and check your answers.**

allowed	needed	obliged	should	required	supposed

1 I'm not sure. In my school, students weren't ______ to attend classes.

2 I don't think students should be ______ to go to classes or to study certain subjects.

3 Well, in many cases people took subjects and exams earlier than they were ______ to.

4 We weren't ______ to have dirty shoes.

5 That's clearly unreasonable. The punishment ______ fit the crime.

6 You quickly learned what you ______ to do.

B WORK IT OUT Choose the correct options to complete the rules.

obligation, prohibition and permission

Strong obligation

We use *have to, must, need to, be obliged to, be required to* to talk about things that [1]***are necessary / aren't necessary***.

Lack of obligation

We use *don't have to, don't need to, be not obliged to, be not required to* to talk about things that [2]***are necessary / aren't necessary***.

Weak obligation

We use *should, be supposed to* to talk about things that [3]***are recommended / aren't recommended***.

Prohibition

We use *must not, can't, be not allowed to* to talk about things that [4]***are permitted / aren't permitted***.

Permission

We use *can, let* or *be allowed to* to talk about things that [5]***are permitted / aren't permitted***.

C Go to the Grammar Hub on page VI.

D PRACTICE Choose the correct options (a, b or c) to complete the sentences.

1 My parents didn't ___ me go out alone until I was 18.
a require **b** need **c** let

2 I'm going to ___ my children have a lot more freedom than I had.
a let **b** allow **c** need

3 I was ___ do a lot of housework, but usually I didn't bother.
a allowed to **b** need to **c** supposed to

4 I ___ practice the piano for an hour every day. I hated it!
a didn't have to **b** could **c** had to

5 I think people ___ be allowed to drive at 16. You can work then, so having a car would help.
a should **b** have to **c** must

6 We ___ study a foreign language. I think it was a mistake, because languages are important.
a had to **b** didn't have to **c** must not

E SPEAK Work in pairs. Change the sentences in Exercise D so they are true for you.

PRONUNCIATION

Intonation to show interest

6.3 **A Listen to this exchange from the radio show. What kind of intonation does Jessica use to show interest: rise (↗), fall (↘) or rise-fall (↗↘)?**

Andrew: We had to wear a tag around our neck with a message such as 'I have 24 hours to straighten up my uniform' if we looked sloppy. If we behaved badly in class, we had to study on our own. We were forced to do this for five classes. Hundreds of children had to do this. I have similar rules in my school.

Jessica: You're joking! How embarrassing!

6.4 **B Listen to the same exclamations said in two different ways. For each exclamation, choose the speaker (a or b) that shows the most interest.**

1 How embarrassing! a / b
2 Interesting! a / b
3 That's ridiculous! a / b
4 That's amazing! a / b
5 What a nightmare! a / b

C Write down three interesting facts about yourself.

D SPEAK Work in pairs. Take turns telling each other your facts from Exercise C. Use intonation to express interest. Then ask follow-up questions for more information.

SPEAKING

A PREPARE Work in pairs. Think about all of your previous schools. Discuss rules that you didn't like and why.

A: At my elementary school, anyone that forgot their uniform had to do the whole class in their underwear!
B: Really? How embarrassing!

B PLAN Work in pairs. Make a list of five rules for the perfect school, for both students and teachers. Use your ideas from Exercise A to help you.

C PRESENT Present your rules to the class. Explain your reasons for each.

Our first rule is simple – students must be given a say in the topics and subjects they cover. We think that …

D DISCUSS As a class, discuss how to improve your language school. Would any of the rules from Exercise C improve your school experience?

VOCABULARY
Education

A Look at the infographic. Complete the definitions with the words in bold.

1 ________________ (n) a school that is free because it is funded by the government

2 ________________ (n) a school that you pay money to attend

3 ________________ (n) a school where students also live full-time

4 ________________ (adj) something that must be done because of rules or laws

5 ________________ (n) education at a university or at a college of a similar level

6 ________________ (n) the subjects studied in a school, college, etc.

EDUCATION
AROUND THE GLOBE

With fees of about $133,000 a year, *Le Rosey* in Switzerland is the world's most expensive **private school**.

Wearing a school uniform isn't **compulsory** in most high schools in the US, although there is usually a fairly strict dress code.

State schools in France have one of the shortest school years with nearly 4 months of vacation, but the longest school day in the world with up to 40 hours a week in the final years.

A lot of the **curriculum** in Canadian schools is taught in both English and French.

England is home to the world's oldest **boarding school**. Students have lived and studied in The King's School since 597 CE.

According to the Organization for Economic Co-operation and Development, 66% of students in Finland go into **higher education** to get a degree. This is the highest rate in Europe.

B Go to the Vocabulary Hub on page XVI.

C SPEAK Work in groups. Discuss the questions.

1 At what age do people start elementary school in your country? Do you think this is the right age? Why/Why not?

2 Would you send your children to private school if you could afford it? Why/Why not?

3 Which subjects are compulsory in your country?

4 Do you think higher education should be provided for free? Why/Why not?

5 Do you think lectures are an effective way to learn? Why/Why not?

READING

A (6.5) Listen to an interview about a new movie. When is it set? Who does the actress play in the movie?

B (6.5) Listen again. Complete the summary of school life in the period with no more than three words from the interview.

Most children used to [1]________________ and didn't go to school. Some [2]________________ boys could get scholarships but not girls. Girls from rich families sometimes went to boarding school, but most were taught at [3]________________ by a governess. A governess was a little like a [4]________________.

C PREDICT Work in pairs. You're going to read an adapted extract from Anne Brontë's novel *Agnes Grey*. What do you think might be hard for her as the governess of two young rich children?

D SCAN Read the extract and check your predictions from Exercise B.

Agnes Grey

Teaching and looking after the children became harder, rather than easier, as I got to know them. Master Tom not only refused to be controlled but tried to control me and his sister. He often refused to do his lessons. Sometimes I had to sit with my chair against the door in order to keep him in the schoolroom. At last, after trying to push me out of the way, and making faces at me, he would finally do his work.

Tom, however, was not as bad a pupil as Mary Ann. If I asked her to read a book or do some writing, she would drop to the floor and yell loudly. She was too heavy for me to pick her up and she would lie there until the lunch bell meant she could escape. Then she would jump up with a big smile on her face. She knew she had won.

In desperation, I decided that I should focus on two very important things in order to change their behaviour. I had to be patient and I had to be strict. So, I focused on doing this with all my strength over the coming weeks. However, it did not matter how hard I tried. Their behaviour did not get any better.

I will never forget one cold snowy January afternoon. The children had come into the schoolroom, shouting that they planned 'to be naughty,' and they had done exactly that. Mary Ann took my bag and started to look at what was inside it. When she saw that it only contained my work papers and books, she threw it on the fire! I ran to the other side of the room and pulled the bag out of the fire. Then Tom jumped up from his chair and yelled, 'Let's throw her desk out of the window!' He grabbed my desk, which contained my letters and what little money I owned. I quickly went to rescue it. Both children then ran away from me, out of the house and into the snow, where they rolled about shouting with happiness.

E PRONOUN REFERENCING **Read the extract again. Match the pronouns (1–8) to the people or things they refer to. Use the information in the box to help you.**

Pronoun referencing

Writers frequently use pronouns to refer backward and forward to different ideas in a text. These help to make the text more organized and the language more varied for the reader. Identifying what ideas these pronouns refer to will help you to understand a text better.

1 them (line 2) ________
2 him (line 6) ________
3 her (line 10) ________
4 she (line 10) ________
5 their (line 17) ________
6 this (line 19) ________
7 that (line 25) ________
8 it (line 26) ________

F SPEAK **Work in groups. Discuss the questions.**

1 In the first paragraph, Tom is described as 'making faces' at Agnes. What do you think this means?
2 What do you think Agnes could have done differently to control Tom and Mary Ann's behavior?
3 In the novel *Agnes Grey*, the children are allowed to choose when they study. Do you think this is a good idea? Why/Why not?

SPEAKING HUB

A PLAN **Think about how education has changed in your country over the past 50 years. Write notes about:**

- discipline
- subjects
- age of starting/leaving education
- college

B SPEAK **Work in pairs. Use your notes to discuss changes in your country. What are the main differences between 50 years ago and now?**

C DISCUSS **Work in groups. Discuss the questions.**

1 Has education in your country improved over the past 50 years? Why/Why not?
2 What would you change about the current education system in your country?
3 Is there anything from 50 years ago that you'd like to reintroduce to the current system?

Discuss rules in education
Talk about changes to education in your country

6.2 Traditions of youth

- Discuss age milestones in your country
- Debate the best time to start college

G – articles
V – compound adjectives; phrases with *make* and *do*
P – intrusive /j/ sounds
S – decoding: idioms

READING

A SPEAK **Work in pairs. Discuss the questions.**

1 At what age do you think someone becomes an adult? Why?
2 What events or celebrations happen in your country to show that someone is becoming an adult?

B SCAN **Read *Coming of age* quickly. Match the ages (1–3) to the things they represent (a–c).**

1	7 or 8	a	When you can learn to drive and leave school in the US.
2	20	b	When childhood is over in Vanuatu.
3	16	c	When someone becomes an adult in Japan.

C READ FOR DETAIL **Read the article again and answer the questions. Underline the parts of the text that give you the answers.**

1 In Vanuatu, what do mothers hold when their children complete their first jump? What happens to the item?
2 Which official venue do participants visit during the *Seijin-no-Hi* celebrations?
3 What traditions are associated with Sweet 16 celebrations?
4 What does giving a car to someone on their 16th birthday represent in the US and Canada?

D SPEAK **Work in groups. What other coming-of-age ceremonies do you know of? What happens in them?**

GRAMMAR

Articles

A **Complete the extracts with *a, an, the* or – (no article). Then scan the article again to check your answers.**

1 They traditionally signify a point in someone's life when ________ childhood is over.
2 In ________ Vanuatu, ________ small island in ________ Pacific Ocean, young boys jump from ________ 30-meter-high tower…
3 The vine is cut to a length that will just stop them from hitting ________ ground…
4 It is ________ ancient tradition that started almost 1,300 years ago.
5 In recent years, ________ popularity of ________ festival has declined…
6 Sweet 16 is the term given to ________ coming-of-age party to celebrate ________ teenager's 16th birthday.

COMING OF AGE

Coming-of-age events are important in many cultures. They traditionally signify a point in someone's life when childhood is over. Immediately afterward, the person is considered to have a different role within society. However, from shows of strength and bravery to simply having a big party, these life-changing events vary greatly throughout the world.

VANUATU LAND DIVE

Thrillseekers will love this high-risk ceremony! In Vanuatu, a small island in the Pacific Ocean, young boys jump from a 30-meter-high tower, with a bungee-like vine tied to their ankles. The vine is cut to a length that will just stop them from hitting the ground, but, unlike a bungee rope, it isn't elastic!

From the age of seven or eight boys are allowed to jump from a smaller tower. During their first few dives, their mothers hold an item which represents their childhood. Once they have completed the jump, the item is thrown away to symbolize that their childhood has ended. As they grow older, boys jump from taller towers to show their manliness to their community.

SWEET 16

Sweet 16 is the name given to the coming-of-age party to celebrate a teenager's 16th birthday. It doesn't have a long history and there are no specific traditions to follow. However, it has grown in popularity in the US and Canada in recent years. The concept became well-known when MTV launched a show called *My Super Sweet Sixteen*, in which cameras followed parents spending hundreds of thousands of dollars on elaborate parties for their children, who wanted the biggest and best party in town.

In most states,16 is also the age when people can leave school and when they can start to drive. As a result, one tradition that has developed is the gift of a car. This symbolizes the person's increased freedom and responsibility as they become older.

SEIJIN-NO-HI

The coming-of-age festival called *Seijin-no-Hi* is held in Japan on the second Monday of January. It is an ancient tradition that started almost 1,300 years ago. The festival symbolizes the point at which the Japanese believe people become mature members of society – 20 years old. It is also the age at which they are permitted to vote.

During the day, 20-year-olds taking part dress up in their finest traditional clothes and attend a ceremony in local city offices. Government officials give speeches and small gifts are handed out. These young adults then go on to celebrate at parties in the evening. In recent years, the popularity of the festival has declined and many have stayed away from the celebrations.

B WORK IT OUT Complete the rules with the titles in the box.

definite article (*the*) | indefinite article (*a/an*) | zero article (-)

Articles

[1]We use the ______________________:
- when we talk about something for the first time
- when it's not clear or important which one of a group is being talked about

[2]We use the ______________________:
- when there's only one of something
- when it's clear which thing we're talking about (usually because we've mentioned it before)
- with superlatives
- with rivers, some mountains, oceans, seas, plural country names, groups of islands and deserts

[3]We use the ______________________:
- to talk about things in general
- with most towns, cities, countries, continents, states, lakes and mountains

C Go to the **Grammar Hub** on **page VI**.

D PRACTICE Work in pairs. Student A – Go to the **Communication Hub** on **page XIX**. Student B – Go to the **Communication Hub** on **page XX**.

E SPEAK Work in pairs. Tell your partner about the coming-of-age ceremony you have just read about.

PRONUNCIATION
Intrusive /j/ sounds

6.6 **A** Listen to the sentence below. Notice the /j/ sound that appears between the words connected with a (‿).

The‿American legal system is complex, and laws vary from state to state. Depending on the state, the‿age you can get a full drivers licence is anywhere between 16 and 18 years old.

6.7 **B** Read the sentences below. Draw a (‿) between any words that you think are connected by a /j/ sound. Then listen and check.

1 The average age to drive a car in most countries is 18.
2 In Bangladesh, many children leave the education system at ten years old.
3 You can vote in Scotland from the age of 16.
4 In the UK, the older generation could leave school at 14.

VOCABULARY
Compound adjectives

Compound adjectives

Compound adjectives are single adjectives formed from two (or more) words. Many are joined with a hyphen (-), especially when they come before a noun.

Compound adjectives can:
- include numbers, e.g. *30-meter-high*
- use participles, e.g. *old-fashioned, well-known*
- have multiple parts, e.g. *coming-of-age*
- combine adjectives and nouns, e.g. *high-risk*

Do not add an *s* to compound adjectives with numbers, (e.g. *30-meter-high* not ~~*30-meters-high*~~).

Complete the sentences with the compound adjectives in the box.

coming-of-age | last-minute | old-fashioned | seven-bedroom | up-to-date | well-known

1 For the most ________________ information on flights, please visit our website.
2 My parents have some pretty ________________ ideas about raising children.
3 Apparently, he just bought a huge ________________ house outside Houston.
4 It's a ________________ movie about three young friends growing up together.
5 I'm going to be late because there was a ________________ change to the schedule.
6 We've booked a ________________ author to speak at next month's event.

SPEAKING

A PLAN Write notes on the age people can do these things in your country. Do you think these are the right ages? Why/Why not?

- leave school
- drive a car
- start work
- retire

B DISCUSS Work in groups. What do you think is the best age for each of the things in Exercise A? Try to agree on one age for each.

C PRESENT Tell the class the ages you chose for each event and explain your reasons.

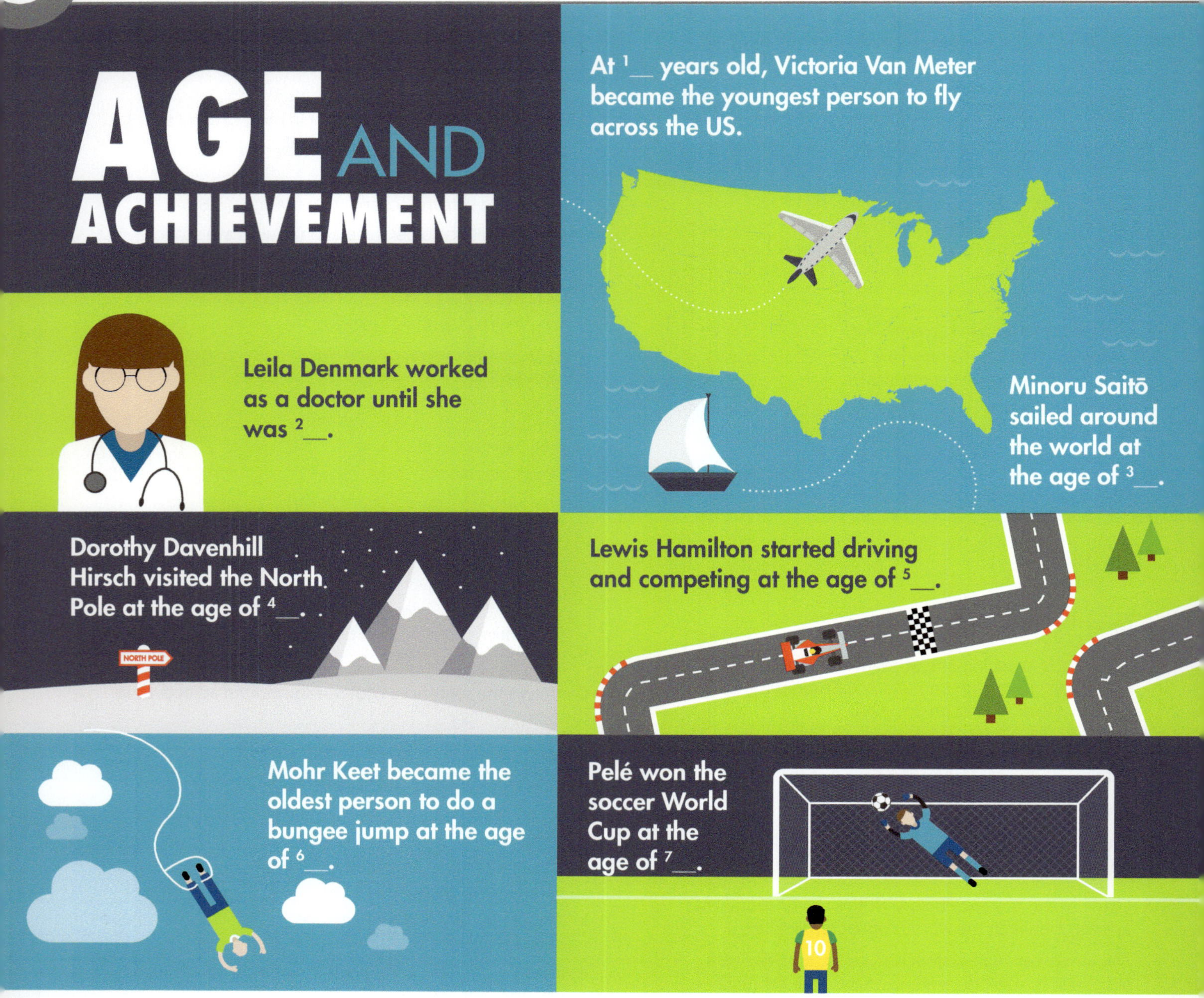

LISTENING

A PREDICT Predict when the achievements in the infographic were accomplished, using the ages in the box.

8	11	17	77	89	96	103

B COMPARE Work in pairs. Compare your predictions from Exercise A. Explain your reasoning.

C SPEAK Work in pairs. Discuss the questions.

1. What do you think motivated each person?
2. What difficulties do you think they might have faced?
3. What were you doing / What do you think you'll be doing at each age?

D DISCUSS Work in groups. Discuss the questions.

1. You are going to listen to three interviews from a TV show called *Age is just a number*. What do you think the title means? Do you agree with this idea?
2. The interviewees talk about achievements at the ages of 14, 28 and 70. What key events usually happen at these ages?

6.8 **E LISTEN FOR GIST** Listen and match the speakers (1–3) to an achievement (a–d). One achievement is not mentioned.

Speaker 1	**a** getting into college
Speaker 2	**b** winning a competition
Speaker 3	**c** starting their own company
	d getting over a fear

6.8 **F LISTEN FOR DETAIL Listen to the interviews again and answer the questions. Use the information in the box to help you.**

> **Decoding: idioms**
>
> Idioms (e.g. *a blessing in disguise, blood is thicker than water*, etc) are frequently used in informal spoken English. They can be difficult to understand because their meaning is different from the meaning of the individual words. To help with this, listen for contextual clues before and after the idiom.

1 How did Janice feel about starting her business?
  - a She felt very confident.
  - b She was worried but pushed herself to do it.
  - c She started it without really thinking.

2 How successful is Janice's business?
  - a She's making a lot of money.
  - b She's making a reasonable amount of money.
  - c She's losing money.

3 What does Kayley say about school?
  - a It was challenging.
  - b It was boring.
  - c It was easy.

4 How did Robbie's wife feel about their honeymoon plans?
  - a She was fine because she understood his fears.
  - b She was angry because she thought his fear was irrational.
  - c She was fine because she wanted to stay in the US.

G SPEAK Work in pairs. Look at the audio script on page XXIX to find the idioms that gave you the answers in Exercise F. Do you have any similar idioms in your country?

VOCABULARY

Phrases with *make* and *do*

6.9 **A Listen and complete the extracts from the interview. What do you think each phrase means?**

1 I used to ______________ and take care of the grandchildren a couple of mornings a week.

2 They ______________, they were just full of energy.

3 Well, you know… it's hard but I'm ______________ ______________.

4 I think schools should ______________ age restrictions for taking exams.

5 People are generally nice, and I think they'll ______________ ______________ for my age.

6 I hope I ______________, but I am a little worried.

7 She was trying to [a] ______________ the situation by [b] ______________ the exciting honeymoon…

B Match the phrases in Exercise A (1–7) to their definitions (a–h).

a to be positive about a situation you don't like but can't change 7a

b to succeed in living or working without someone or something ___

c something that you do for someone in order to help them ___

d to get rid of something ___

e try to make something work ___

f causing no serious damage or injury ___

g to consider the reasons for somebody's behavior and not judge them too severely ___

h to make other people notice you in a positive way ___

C Complete the questions with the correct form of the phrases in Exercise A.

1 Do you ignore people's age, or do you think you ______________ for people because of their age?

2 When you ______________ for someone, do you expect them to do something in return?

3 Does eating junk food occasionally ______________?

4 Is there a time in your life when you had to ______________ a difficult situation?

5 Since my business is failing in its first year, should I keep ______________ to make it work or close it?

6 Should governments ______________ unemployment pay and benefits?

7 What's the best way to ______________ on others?

8 What would be the hardest thing to ______________ for a year?

D SPEAK Work in pairs. Discuss the questions in Exercise C.

SPEAKING HUB

A PLAN Work in pairs. What are the advantages and disadvantages of going to college right after you leave high school?

B PREPARE Work in two groups. You are going to debate the following:

Most teenagers don't know what career they want when they finish high school. Instead of making such a big decision at 18, they should work or travel for at least a year before going to college.

Group A – You agree with the idea above.

Group B – You disagree with the idea above.

Plan your arguments. Think about how to support your position, as well as what the other group might say.

C SPEAK Hold your debate.

Discuss age milestones in your country
Debate the best time to start college

A floating school

COMPREHENSION

A Work in pairs. Look at the picture and discuss the questions.

1 What kind of building do you think it is? Why?
2 Do you think it's temporary or permanent? Why?
3 Where do you think it is?

B Watch a news report about the building in Exercise A and check your answers.

C Watch the news report again. Choose the correct options (a, b or c) to answer the questions.

1 What does the reporter mean when he says that 'water is in the blood' of these children?
   a They are used to living and working on the water.
   b Their parents expect them to become fishermen.
   c They never travel to the mainland.
2 What does the reporter mean when he says the school is 'widening horizons' for the children?
   a It provides them with the chance to travel.
   b It provides them with a unique view of their community.
   c It provides them with more opportunities in life.
3 Which of the following doesn't the reporter describe on his tour of the school?
   a the number of students
   b the conditions in the classroom
   c the view from the classroom
4 Which sentence best describes the school's founder?
   a His father was the oldest of 22 children and the first to get an education.
   b He is the youngest of 22 children and the first to get an education.
   c He is the father of 22 children and the first to get an education.

D Work in groups. Discuss the questions.

1 What do you think the reporter means when he says, 'What the community lacks in glamour, it makes up for in grit'?
2 What do you think the reporter means when he says, 'the school has given students the opportunity to think big'?

AUTHENTIC ENGLISH

A Work in pairs. Read the extract from the video. What type of clause is used at the beginning of the sentence? How does this affect the emphasis?

What's unique about this classroom is that it's open air.

B Read the information in the box and check your answers to Exercise A.

Emphatic structures

Speakers frequently emphasize a specific part of a sentence by building up to it with an essential adjective clause. Beginning the clause with *What* puts the emphasis on the information after *be*.

What's really interesting about the school is the location. (= the emphasis is on *the location*)

We can also use *the thing that*, *the* + adj + *thing* and *all I* + verb to achieve the same effect.

The most impressive thing at my school was the main hall.

All I wanted to do was play soccer, not study!

C Work in pairs. Take turns completing the sentences (1–5) with your own ideas.

1 What's unique about my hometown is …
2 What I don't miss about school is …
3 The thing that I worry about most is …
4 The interesting thing about my country is …
5 All I want for my birthday this year is …

SAM MALCOLM AMANDA HARRY EMILY

Who are you talking to?

A Work in pairs. Discuss what you think makes a good presentation. Explain your reasoning.

B Watch the video and answer the questions.

1 What has Malcolm agreed to help Harry with?
2 Why is he qualified to do this?
3 Does Harry improve with Malcolm's help?

SPEAKING SKILL

A Watch the video again. What does Malcolm think is the main issue with Harry's presentation?

B Look at the two different versions of Harry's introduction. Identify the informal and formal features. Use the information in the box to help you.

1 Hey guys! How's things? So glad you were able to drop by for my little chat today. I'm gonna be talking 'bout some of the cool ideas that people have come up with for teaching kids in developing countries. I'll be letting you know if I think they're any good and …

2 Thank you for coming to my presentation today. I am going to be talking about some of the educational innovations that governments and individuals have devised for teaching children in developing countries. I will be assessing these on their effectiveness and …

Using correct register

Informal register

We generally use an informal register when we are talking to our friends and family. Some common features of an informal register are:

- Shortened sentences – *~~(I'm)~~ so glad you were able to …*
- Phrasal verbs – *OK if we quickly run through this presentation now?*
- Slang – *Cheers, dude.*
- Idioms – *… he'll give me a hand …, OK if I take five?*
- Abbreviations – *… I've seen it on TV.*

Formal register

In addition to avoiding the features listed above, we frequently use less direct language when we are being formal, such as *I would be grateful if you could …, I was wondering if I might …, I'm sorry, but I'm afraid …*

C Work in pairs. Why is it important to adapt your register to your audience?

D Work in pairs. Student A – Do one of the following in an informal register. Student B – Say the same thing in a formal register. Then swap.

- Ask your partner if you can do something.
- Offer something to your partner.
- Refuse an invitation from your partner.
- Apologize to your partner for something.

A: Shut the window, will you?
B: Excuse me, I was just wondering if I could ask you to close the window?

SPEAKING HUB

A PREPARE Work in pairs. Choose one of the topics to give a presentation about. Write notes.

- the right time to go to college
- school rules and discipline
- different school systems

B PLAN Organize your notes from Exercise A into a plan for a formal presentation.

C PRESENT Work in groups. Give your presentation and answer any questions.

D DISCUSS Work in new pairs. Tell your partner what you learned in the presentations using an informal register.

Give your opinion on an aspect of education

➤ Turn to page XXIII to learn how to write a report.

Unit 6 Review

VOCABULARY

A Choose the correct options (a, b or c) to complete the sentences.

1 The fees for my ___ are $20,000 a year.
   a state school
   b private school
   c higher education
2 More and more people are staying in ___ until they complete a master's degree.
   a higher education
   b graduate
   c campus
3 There were over 500 students in my ___ on International Management today because we had an exam.
   a curriculum
   b seminar
   c lecture
4 The university has its own ___ that you need to pass to get in.
   a entrance exam
   b scholarship
   c seminar
5 My sister has won a ___ to a top college.
   a scholarship
   b seminar
   c graduate
6 I'd like to do a ___ course in something like electronics.
   a compulsory
   b curriculum
   c vocational

B Work in groups. Discuss the questions.

1 Would you rather stay on campus while in college or commute from home? Why?
2 Which subjects do you think should be added/removed from the school curriculum in your country? Why?

C Complete the second sentence so it has a similar meaning to the first, using the words in bold.

1 They've just moved into a house with three bedrooms.
   three-bedroom
   They've just moved ______________________________.
2 The décor in this restaurant isn't very modern.
   old-fashioned
   The décor ______________________________.
3 The author Haruki Murakami is well known in Japan.
   well-known
   Haruki Murakami is a ______________________________.
4 Isaac's commute takes two hours!
   two-hour
   Isaac has ______________________________.

D Match the numbers (1–8) to the letters (a–h) to form full sentences.

1 I'm not happy with my apartment but I'm trying to ...
2 We've been trying ...
3 Can you ...
4 I think you need to make ...
5 Just one soda a day isn't going to ...
6 What do you think of this suit? I want to ...
7 It's hard living in a new city but I'm ...
8 This new system will allow us ...

a do me a favor?
b do any harm.
c make the best of it.
d doing my best.
e make a good impression.
f allowances for his lack of experience.
g to do without a car for the last month.
h to do away with a lot of paperwork.

GRAMMAR

A Choose the correct options to complete the sentences.

1 I was ***supposed to*** / ***required to*** finish it by five but I can't be bothered.
2 You ***don't need to*** / ***must not*** bring anything to the party but you can if you want to.
3 I think you ***'re required to*** / ***should*** complain to the manager. You might get a refund.
4 We ***must not*** / ***needn't*** leave any garbage or we'll get fined.
5 You ***are required to*** / ***should*** show ID or they won't let you in.
6 We ***aren't allowed to*** / ***should*** accept gifts from our clients or we could get in trouble.
7 You really ***are required to*** / ***need to*** drink more water when it's this hot!
8 You ***aren't supposed to*** / ***can't*** smoke in public buildings. It's against the law.

B Work in pairs. Discuss any rules or obligations in your school or work that you'd like to change and why.

C Complete the sentences with *a, an, the* or – (no article).

1 _______ education should be free for everyone.
2 Did you go to _______ movies last night?
3 He ran seven marathons through _______ Sahara Desert.
4 I'll meet you on _______ Main Street at seven.
5 Do you have _______ address for the apartment?
6 Do you have _______ signal on your phone?
7 We're having _______ party to celebrate his 21st birthday.
8 _______ Germany went out of the World Cup in the group stages.

7 COMMUNITY

> A community is like a ship; everyone ought to be prepared to take the helm.
>
> Henrik Ibsen

A group of young community farmers displaying the produce of their shared allotment.

OBJECTIVES

- discuss community development projects
- discuss responses to hypothetical situations
- talk about wishes and regrets
- design and present a community project
- give your opinion on a social initiative
- write a formal letter of complaint

Work with a partner. Discuss these questions.

1 Read the quote. What do you think Ibsen means? Do you agree with him? Why/Why not?

2 What do you do to help people in your local community?

3 What do you like most about where you live?

7.1 Open spaces

- Discuss community development projects
- Discuss responses to hypothetical situations

G – first conditional with different future forms; unreal conditionals
S – identifying speculation
V – verbs to describe change
P – connected speech in conditionals

LISTENING

A SPEAK **Work in groups. Look at the picture and discuss the questions.**

1 Are there any buildings like this in your town or city?
2 What were they originally used for? What are they used for now?
3 What do you think would be a better use of the space?
4 Is it better to repurpose them or knock them down? Why?

7.1 **B LISTEN FOR MAIN IDEA** **Listen to the talk. Match the original spaces to what they are used for now and the main reason for the change.**

	Original space	New use	Main reason for the change
1	industrial estate	art gallery	to inspire local children
2	warehouse	community garden	to educate local children
3	wasteland	community park	to tackle obesity

C SPEAK **Work in pairs. Summarize what you remember about each of the projects. Use the information in Exercise B to help you.**

7.1 **D LISTEN FOR DETAIL** **Listen to the talk again. Are these sentences true (T) or false (F)? Correct the false sentences.**

1 Originally, the industrial estate was going to be used for offices. *T / F*
2 The park gives many urban children their first taste of nature. *T / F*
3 The gallery exhibits artwork inspired by the city. *T / F*
4 Local schools can exhibit work twice a year. *T / F*
5 Many people don't eat fresh produce because of the expense. *T / F*
6 All the food from the garden is given to homeless people. *T / F*

E SPEAK **Work in groups. Would any of the regeneration projects described in the talk work well in your town or city? Why/Why not?**

GRAMMAR

First conditional with different future forms

7.2 **A** **Listen and complete the extracts with the correct form of the verbs in parentheses.**

1 In fact, if we ____________ (*maintain*) our current numbers, we ____________ (*have*) 15,000 visitors in our first year.
2 If we ____________ (*give*) kids opportunities like this, what ____________ (*they / achieve*) in the future?
3 If you ____________ (*think*) about starting a garden, ____________ (*speak*) to me later.
4 If we ____________ (*not come*) together as a community, neighborhoods like mine ____________ (*fall*) apart.
5 If you ____________ (*care*) about your community, ____________ (*do*) something to improve it.

B WORK IT OUT **Choose the correct options to complete the rules.**

> **First conditional with different future forms**
>
> We use the first conditional to talk about something that is possible in the [1]***past / future***.
>
> We can use any [2]***present / future*** tense in the *if*-clause and any [3]***present / future*** tense or an imperative in the main clause.

C Go to the **Grammar Hub** on **page VIII**.

D PRACTICE Choose the correct options to complete the sentences.

1 If everything goes according to plan, ***we'll have opened* / *we'll open*** a total of 20 community gardens in the city by 2020.

2 We're going to convert this old factory into a skate park if ***we get* / *we'll get*** the funding.

3 If they don't hurry up, the project ***isn't* / *won't be*** finished on time.

4 ***We'll be looking* / *We'll have looked*** at the plans tomorrow if you want to come along.

5 If you go to the meeting, ***ask* / *to ask*** the residents how they feel.

6 If ***they're growing* / *they'll be growing*** their own vegetables, they should sell them, too.

VOCABULARY

Verbs to describe change

A Read *Transforming Main Street*. Complete the definitions with the words in bold.

1 ________________ to make longer or bigger

2 ________________ to move to another place

3 ________________ to change the use of something

4 ________________ to knock down or destroy

5 ________________ to repair something so that it looks the same as it did originally

6 ________________ to build or make something like a building, road or machine

7 ________________ to change something completely

Home News Contact

Transforming Main Street

Our main priority is to **transform** the public spaces in the city center.

We need to encourage large chains to **relocate** to the city center to make Main Street a thriving shopping area again.

The next most important thing is to deal with the former industrial area. There is the potential to **convert** this into residential properties, stores, cafés and restaurants. We should **demolish** some of the worst buildings but **restore** any of historical interest.

To make this development a success, we will need to **extend** the blue subway line into the area and **construct** new schools for the residents' children.

B Complete the questions with the correct form of the verbs in Exercise A.

1 Do you think it's better to ________________ old buildings or ________________ them to make way for new ones? Why?

2 What is one change that would completely ________________ your hometown for the better?

3 Your hometown wants to ________________ a new road through a local park. How would you feel?

4 What could old unused Main Street stores be ________________ into now that most people shop online?

5 Why do you think so many stores ________________ from the main street to out-of-town shopping malls?

6 Do you think it is better to ________________ public transportation to all parts of a city or to encourage more bike riding? Why?

C Work in pairs. Discuss the questions in Exercise B.

SPEAKING

A PREPARE Work in pairs. Look at the map of an abandoned area and discuss the main issues.

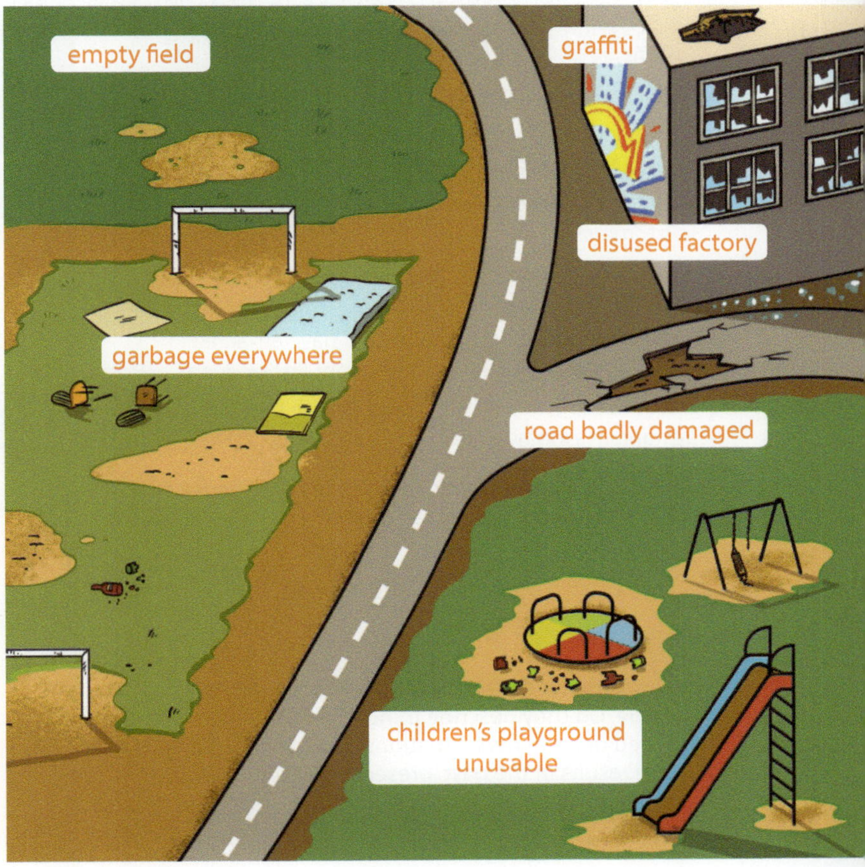

B PLAN Work in groups. Discuss how the area could be improved for the local community. Agree on three changes to make and rank them in order of importance.

I think the easiest area to address is the park. If we clean up the garbage, children will have somewhere to play soccer.

C PRESENT Present your ideas to the class. Explain your reasoning.

READING

A SPEAK Work in pairs. Discuss the questions.

1 What are the most important elements of a successful restaurant?

2 Why do you think so many restaurants close within their first year?

B SCAN Scan *It could have been so much better ...* quickly. What is it about?

1 The rise and fall of China Garden.

2 Why you shouldn't start a business.

3 Why China Garden is failing.

C IDENTIFY SPECULATION Read the article again and answer the questions. Underline the parts of the text that gives you the answers. Use the information in the box to help you.

> **Identifying speculation**
>
> Speculation is when someone guesses reasons behind something without necessarily having all the facts, e.g. *I don't know ... maybe it's the right restaurant, but just the wrong location.*

1 Why does Mei Lù think the business is failing?

2 What does Mario Coniglio believe makes the chefs' standard of cooking lower?

3 What does he feel creates a bad atmosphere for the customers?

4 What would encourage Nicki Wright to eat at China Garden more frequently?

5 What does Alex Mullins feel would have attracted more customers when the restaurant first opened?

6 What does he think the problem is with the restaurant's ingredients?

D SPEAK Work in pairs. What are the top three issues you think the owner needs to address?

GRAMMAR

Unreal conditionals

A Work in pairs. Read the following sentences from the article. Do they describe things that actually happened or imaginary situations? Do they describe possible results in the past, present or future?

1 If I hadn't set up China Garden, I would have continued working in an office job that I hated for the rest of my life.

2 If there was less competition in the area, I think the business would be much more successful.

3 If they'd spent more money on promotion in the area, more people would know about the restaurant.

B WORK IT OUT Match the sentences (1–3) in Exercise A to the rules (a–c).

> **Unreal conditionals**
>
> **a Second conditional** ___
>
> We use *if* + simple past + *would/might/could* + base form to talk about the consequences of an imagined present or future.
>
> **b Third conditional** ___
>
> We use *if* + past perfect and *would/might/could* + *have* + past participle to talk about the past consequences of a hypothetical, different past.
>
> **c Mixed conditionals** ___
>
> We can use a mixture of the second and third conditional by using *if* + past perfect + *would/might/could* + base form. This is used to imagine the present consequences of a hypothetical, different past.

C Go to the **Grammar Hub** on **page VIII**.

IT COULD HAVE BEEN SO MUCH BETTER ...

In New York, there are hundreds of good Chinese restaurants already in existence, so establishing a new one is always going to be extremely challenging. China Garden is a family-run restaurant selling Chinese and Asian fusion food in New York's Chinatown. However, the restaurant is in trouble. Last year it lost almost $300,000. If things continue in the same way, the restaurant won't be there in six months.

When we met with the owner, Mei Lù, she was understandably not in a very positive mood. 'I always wanted to run my own restaurant. If I hadn't set up China Garden, I would have continued working in an office job that I hated for the rest of my life. But now I'm really starting to regret the decision. If there was less competition in the area, I think the business would be much more successful. I don't know ... Maybe it's the right restaurant, but just the wrong location.' So, is Mei right? Did she just set up business in the wrong part of the city or are there other reasons behind the restaurant's poor performance? We spoke to the staff, locals and critics to dig a little deeper.

Mario Coniglio has been the head waiter at China Garden since it opened last July. Despite the competition, he thinks the location is fine, but the number of items on the menu is having a negative effect on the business. 'The menu is enormous, and a lot of customers seem to find it difficult to know where to start. If we had fewer options, customers could choose more easily. Also, our chefs could probably

D PRACTICE **Complete the sentences with the correct form of the verbs in parentheses. Use contractions where possible.**

1 If I started a business, it ___________ (*be*) in IT because I have a lot of ideas in that area.
2 If I saw someone committing a crime, I ___________ (*stop*) it myself because it's too dangerous. I ___________ (*call*) the police.
3 If I had a lot of money, I ___________ (*buy*) a sports car.
4 I ___________ (*be*) a lot happier now if I hadn't dropped out of college.
5 I ___________ (*work*) much harder if I was paid more.
6 If I hadn't taken my current job, I ___________ (*meet*) my husband.

E SPEAK **Work in pairs. Change the sentences in Exercise D so they are true for you. Ask follow-up questions for more information.**

A: I'd be a lot happier if I hadn't failed my exams.
B: Which exams did you fail?

PRONUNCIATION
Connected speech in conditionals

7.3 **A** **Listen and repeat the clauses. Is there a pause between the words in bold? Is the pronunciation of *have* strong or weak?**

1 Customers **would have** paid more if …
2 Customers **might have** preferred it if …
3 The staff **couldn't have** been friendlier if …

7.4 **B** **Draw a (‿) to show connected speech in the following sentences. Then listen, check and repeat.**

1 I wouldn't have spent the money if I'd known it was such a risk.
2 If the restaurant had been busier, it would have survived longer.
3 If the menu had been simpler, it might have been easier to choose.
4 I think it could have worked if they'd focused more on advertising.

cook to a much higher standard. How can three chefs cook from a menu that has 500 dishes on it? It's crazy!' So, is this the only problem? 'No, I wish it was! Mei gets angry really quickly. It's embarrassing for both the staff and the customers. If she were able to stay a little calmer, the whole atmosphere would be much better.'

It's not only the staff that is unhappy. Customers just don't come back for a second visit. Local food-lover Nicki Wright went to China Garden when it first opened but hasn't been back since. To her, the restaurant simply doesn't offer good value for money. 'The food actually isn't that bad. It's just so much more expensive than other restaurants in the area. If the prices were more competitive, I'd probably eat there more frequently.' The critics also aren't impressed. Alex Mullins, author of the popular food magazine *The Bite*, told us: 'It's a great location. They just didn't do a good job of advertising when they first opened. It's simple. If they'd spent more money on promotion in the area, more people would know about the restaurant. They do need to improve the food as well. It would taste so much better if they used fresh, locally sourced ingredients. The supply is here in New York; they just need to manage the restaurant better.'

While owner Mei Lù blames the location for her restaurant's failure, it's clear that there are many other issues that need to be resolved. While Mei is accepting of some of the criticisms, she strongly disagrees with others, especially the size of the menu. 'We offer customers a wide range of dishes from all over China and beyond. I don't see why that's a problem.'

Whether Mei manages to make a success of her lifelong dream remains to be seen, but one thing is clear – she has a lot more to learn.

SPEAKING HUB

A PREPARE **Read the situations (1–4) and write notes about what you would do in each.**

1 Your dream business is failing. You spent too much money, employed too many friends and borrowed too much from the bank. In order to continue, you need to sell the family home and move into a rented apartment.
2 When you chose your degree in architecture there were a lot of construction jobs in the country. Now the property market has crashed. You have been offered a job as a math teacher.
3 $50,000 was transferred into your bank account by accident. You spent half of the money and the police have arrested you.
4 You left your passwords written in a book in a drawer. Your roommates found it and started posting on your social media for fun. Some of your friends have now unfriended you.

B PLAN **Work in pairs. Discuss your ideas from Exercise A. Try to agree on the best solution for each situation.**

A: If someone posted things through any of my social media accounts, I would shut them all down.
B: Ha ha! Really? I'd just share something embarrassing about them!

C SPEAK **Work with another pair. Explain what you decided in Exercise B and why. Did you agree?**

- Discuss community development projects
- Discuss responses to hypothetical situations

7.2 Make a change

- Talk about wishes and regrets
- Design and present a community project

S – inferring meaning
V – three-part phrasal verbs; compound nouns
G – *wish* and *if only*
P – two-stress phrasal verbs

READING

A SPEAK Work in pairs. Look at the infographic. What regrets do you think people might have in each of these categories?

B SCAN Read the comments. Match each regret to a category in the infographic. Were any of your ideas from Exercise A mentioned?

TOP FIVE

REGRETS IN LIFE

We all have regrets. That job we didn't take. That house we should have bought. However, according to a recent survey by Pulse Media, most people's biggest regrets are connected to – you guessed it – romance, with family coming in a close second. Here are some other interesting results of the survey.

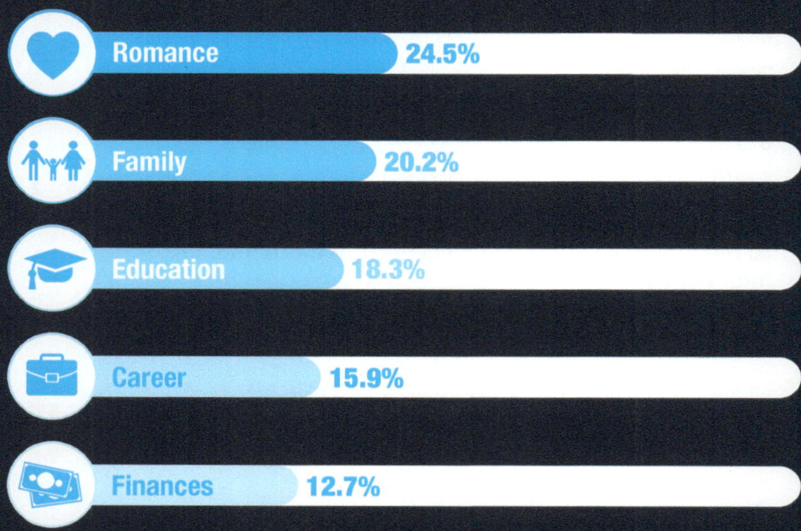

Hayley • 1 hr ago
[1]I wish I hadn't spent so much time worrying about what others thought of me when I was a child. It meant that I forgot to focus on the important issues. If only I'd spent more time studying. [2]I should have gone to a top college, but my grades just weren't good enough. I really feel like I missed out on a massive opportunity.
Reply 5 0

Chris • 1 hr 30 min ago
I'm starting to regret my career choice. I chose a career in finance because I knew I could make a lot of money, but I wish I had chosen a career I enjoyed more. I spend all of Sunday night in a bad mood.
Reply 2 0

Nick • 1 hr 38 min ago
We've recently moved to another town because my dad thinks his career is more important than his family. My mom was happy to move but [3]I wish we still lived in our old town. [4]I wish people wouldn't think only of themselves.
Reply 9 0

Sam • 1 hr 42 min ago
I really wanted to ask out a girl named Maria when I was 16! 🙂 I just used to blush and had no idea what to say to her! I was soooo painfully shy … I wish I had her number now!
Reply 4 0

Christina • 2 hrs ago
My sister and I haven't spoken for two years now. I miss her so much! I'd take back everything I said if I could. I wish she would just pick up the phone and call me.
Reply 1 0

Kelly • 2 hrs 3 mins ago
The last summer of college was one of the happiest times of my life. We traveled so much back then. [5]I wish we could all go back to that beach in Thailand, but everyone's so busy now with work and family. Maybe I wouldn't eat the seafood this time, though!
Reply 3 0

C INFER MEANING **Read the comments again and answer the questions. Use the information in the box to help you.**

Inferring meaning

Writers do not always say directly what they mean. We usually have to use context and our general knowledge to infer meaning.

I chose a career in finance because I knew I could make a lot of money, but I wish I had chosen a career I enjoy more. I spend all of Sunday night in a bad mood.

Here we can infer that the writer spends Sunday night in a bad mood because he doesn't want to go to work the next day.

1 What does Hayley mean by 'the important issues'?
   a being popular
   b getting good grades
   c other people's opinions
2 What massive opportunity did Hayley miss out on?
   a having good friends
   b going to a top college
   c doing well at school
3 Why did Nick's family move?
   a His parents didn't like the old town.
   b His dad got a new job.
   c His mom wanted to move.
4 What happened between Christina and her sister?
   a They never got along.
   b Their parents preferred Christina.
   c They had an argument.
5 What didn't Kelly like about the trip?
   a She got food poisoning.
   b She was on her own.
   c She couldn't find her friends.

D SPEAK **Work in groups. Do you think regrets can ever be beneficial? Why/Why not?**

GRAMMAR
Wish and *if only*

A SPEAK **Work in pairs. Read the comments again. Look at the underlined sentences and answer the questions.**

1 Which sentence describes things that annoy us about other people or things?
2 Which sentences describe regrets about the past?
3 Which sentences describe things we would like to be different in the present or future?

B WORK IT OUT **Complete the box with other examples from the comments.**

wish* and *if only

We use *wish* + simple past to talk about how we would like the present to be different.

a ______________________________

We use *wish* + past perfect to talk about things we regret in the past.

b ______________________________

We use *wish* + object + *would* + base form to talk about something we want others to do or stop doing because it annoys us.

c ______________________________

We can use *if only* instead of *wish* in all of these structures to sound more dramatic or emphatic.

d ______________________________

C **Go to the Grammar Hub on page VIII.**

D PRACTICE **Rewrite the sentences using the words in bold.**

1 It annoys me when people throw garbage on the street.
   wish
   ______________________________.
2 I regret moving to the country.
   wish
   ______________________________.
3 I don't want to work evenings and weekends.
   If only
   ______________________________.
4 I forgot my passport and couldn't go on vacation.
   If only
   ______________________________.
5 It annoys me when people are so rude online.
   wish
   ______________________________.

E SPEAK **Work in pairs. Complete the sentences with your own ideas. Tell your partner. Ask follow-up questions for more information.**

I wish people wouldn't … If only I'd bought …
If I hadn't studied … I wish I were …

SPEAKING

A PREPARE **Write notes about any wishes or regrets you have about the following areas:**

career education family finances romance

B PLAN **Work in pairs. Discuss your wishes and regrets from Exercise A. Which is your biggest regret?**

C DISCUSS **Work in groups. Explain your biggest regrets. What can you learn from them? How could you avoid making the same mistakes in the future?**

LISTENING

A Read the article and answer the questions. Underline the parts of the text that gives you the answers.

1 What is the Freeconomy Community?
2 Why is Mark Boyle called 'the moneyless man'?
3 How did he pay for the farm in Ireland?
4 What system is used on the farm?

7.5 **B LISTEN FOR ORGANIZATION Listen to an interview with someone who started their own Freeconomy Community. Put the topics in the order they are discussed.**

___ starting networking events and workshops to share skills
___ holding community barbecues and street parties
___ starting a website to share goods and skills
___ finding a community site where people can meet
___ finding building materials and people to help

7.5 **C LISTEN FOR DETAIL Listen again. Complete the sentences with no more than three words from the interview.**

1 Callum's experience with one of his ________________ inspired him to set up the Facebook group.
2 They only have a few users but everyone is pretty ________________.
3 They use an old ________________ for their community building.
4 A ________________ gave them their old kitchen equipment to set up a café.
5 They run ________________ events twice a week for people to share their skills.
6 All the food in the café comes from the garden or ________________.

D SPEAK Work in groups. Discuss the questions.

1 How well do you know your neighbors?
2 What kind of community events are there in your area?
3 Would you like to be part of a moneyless community? Why/ Why not?

How We Live

returns for a second series

The popular documentary series *How We Live* returns this month, covering a diverse range of topics from ice fishing in Canada to surfing in Iran.

Episode one focuses on the Irish activist and writer Mark Boyle, best known for establishing the Freeconomy Community – an online network that encourages its members to share skills, tools and land for free. Boyle is commonly referred to as 'the moneyless man', a name he earned by living without money for almost two and a half years. Back in 2008, Boyle quit his job with an organic food company and set up home in a camper he got for free online. Generating electricity via a solar panel he bought for $360, Boyle spent the next few years growing his own food and volunteering on a local farm. In 2010, he published an account of his experience – *The Moneyless Man* – before returning to the monetary world in 2011.

Boyle uses proceeds from the book to purchase land for the Freeconomy Community, including the small farm in County Galway, Ireland, where he currently lives with his partner. The farm, which houses up to 30 volunteers rent free, is based around the idea of 'paying it forward', a system in which one member helps another with the understanding that they will go on to help someone else.

Episode one of How We Live *is available on August 31st.*

VOCABULARY

Three-part phrasal verbs

7.6 **A Complete the sentences with the correct form of the phrasal verbs in the box. Use the definitions in parentheses to help you. Then listen and check.**

come up with	come up against	cut down on
get around to	get along with	look up to

1 Well, obviously I ________________ (*respect and admire*) people like Mark Boyle. He's achieved amazing things.
2 Anyway, luckily, I ________________ (*have a good relationship with someone*) my neighbors and one of them is a professional decorator.
3 Anyway, it turned out he was looking for an accountant, so we ________________ (*think of*) a plan to help us both.
4 So, I set up the Facebook group to give people somewhere to share their skills or give away things they don't want anymore. It actually helps ________________ (*reduce*) waste as well.
5 We had a lot of great ideas that we'd never ________________ (*to finally do something*) working on because we rarely met.
6 It's great because if you ________________ (*to have to deal with something difficult*) a problem, then you can usually find someone here to help.

B Go to the Vocabulary Hub on page XVI.

C Complete the questions with the correct form of the phrasal verbs in the box.

come up against get along with get around to keep up with look up to run out of

1 What things do you regularly want to do but never ______________ doing?
2 Do you think it's important to ______________ your neighbors?
3 Do you have a hero that you ______________?
4 How do you ______________ local news and community events?
5 If you ______________ gas when driving, what would you do?
6 If you ______________ a difficult situation, who do you turn to for help?

D SPEAK Work in pairs. Discuss the questions in Exercise C.

PRONUNCIATION

Two-stress phrasal verbs

7.7 A Listen to the sentences. Which parts of the phrasal verbs are stressed? Circle the main stress. Underline the secondary stress.

1 We need to **come up with** a new way to use the space.
2 People create so much waste trying to **keep up with** the latest trends.
3 We **came up against** many challenges during the project.

7.8 B Listen to each sentence said in two different ways. Choose the sentence that is said with the correct stress on the phrasal verb (a or b).

1 Many old people don't have anyone to **take care of** them. a / b
2 We **teamed up with** the local government and worked on it together. a / b
3 It's a great way to **catch up with** friends. a / b

VOCABULARY

Compound nouns

Compound nouns

A compound noun is a single noun formed from two or more words. The most common type is formed by joining two nouns. For example, *community center*, *project leader*, *skill shortage*, etc.

Match the numbers (1–5) to the letters (a–e) to form compound nouns.

1 We need more **volunteer** …
2 I want to improve my Spanish, so I've joined a **language** …
3 We set up a **car-sharing** …
4 We have opened a **food** …
5 Next week we have organized a **street** …

a **exchange** group.
b **bank** to distribute food to the poor.
c **workers** to help run the youth club.
d **party** in our neighborhood.
e **system** to help reduce pollution and congestion.

SPEAKING HUB

A PREPARE Create a list of skills you could use to help other people. For example, languages, accountancy, design, technology, etc.

B PLAN Work in groups. Discuss your individual skills and decide on a community project you could start together. Write notes about:

- who it will help
- how you will set it up and advertise it
- where it will be based
- what activities you will offer to engage people

C PRESENT Present your project to the class, explaining how it would help the community. Answer their follow-up questions.

Talk about wishes and regrets
Design and present a community project

7.3 A shared vision

A– *you know* S– talking on the telephone

An innovative solution

COMPREHENSION

A Rank the following issues according to how big of a problem they are in your country.

___ house prices
___ cost of living
___ job opportunities
___ street crime
___ corruption
___ access to health care

B Work in pairs. Compare your lists from Exercise A.

Glossary

freehold (n) the legal right to own a building or piece of land for an unlimited period of time

leasehold (n) the legal right to use a building or piece of land for a limited time (as agreed upon in a property contract)

C Watch a news report about a housing project in London and answer the questions.

1 How did the families address the issue of rising house prices?
2 Why is this a cheaper option for them?
3 What other benefits do the residents gain?

D Watch the report again. Are these sentences true (T) or false (F)? Correct the false sentences.

1 The project was part of a housing scheme offered by the local council. *T / F*
2 The houses have turned out to be approximately a fifth cheaper this way. *T / F*
3 The expert believes that properties which share facilities are a better use of land. *T / F*
4 Cressida says she likes how easy it is to socialize with other residents. *T / F*
5 Projects like this could help address housing issues because there is a lot of unused land in the capital. *T / F*

E Work in groups. Do you think community housing projects like this would be effective in your area? Why/Why not?

AUTHENTIC ENGLISH

A Work in pairs. Read the extract from the video. Why do you think the speaker says *you know*?

So you can actually put what are, **you know**, fairly generous houses on quite a small plot of land.

B Read the information in the box and check your answers to Exercise A.

you know

In informal spoken English, we use *you know* for three main reasons:

a To show that what you are referring to is known or understood by the listener.
*Guess who I saw the other day? Juan! **You know**, the guy who used to work on the IT team.*

b To give yourself time to think about what to say next.
*Well, maybe it's time to, **you know**, move on with your life.*

c To emphasize what you're saying.
*It's just so different now, **you know**?*

C Match the sentences (1–3) with the uses in the box (a–c).

1 I was wondering if you'd like to, you know, go and see a movie or something.
2 It's not easy being the only 50-year-old here, you know.
3 What's the name of that movie – you know, the one with Emily Blunt in it?

D Work in pairs. Take turns finishing the sentences with your own ideas.

1 What's the name of that guy in our class? You know, …
2 You know, you really should …
3 We're just going to go shopping and, you know, …

Living together

A Work in pairs. Discuss the questions.

1 Who is the first person you tell when you have big news? Why?

2 Would you ever tell someone something important over the phone or on Skype? Why/Why not?

B Watch the video and answer the questions.

1 Why do you think Amanda's mom mentions Mabel Sanderson at the beginning of the conversation?

2 Why doesn't Amanda's mom like the idea of a shared housing project?

3 What do you think Amanda is thinking when she says, 'you might just be right'?

SPEAKING SKILL

A Complete the box using the phrases below. Then watch the video again to check your answers.

Got to go. I'd better be going ... I need to go
Is it a good time? is that you? I didn't catch that.
that brings me to what I was calling about.
What are you up to? What was that Yes, it's me
You're breaking up.

Talking on the telephone

Phone conversations generally follow a set routine. At the beginning of the conversation, we usually ...

- confirm we're talking to the right person:

Mom: *Oh, Mandy,* [1] ____________________

Amanda: [2] ____________________, *Mom.*

- find out what the person is doing:

Amanda: [3] ____________________

- ask if they are free to talk:

Amanda: [4] ____________________

After exchanging greetings, we usually give a reason for calling:

Amanda: *Actually,* [5] ____________________

Having discussed the reason for calling, we try to bring the conversation to an end:

Amanda: [6] ____________________

Amanda: *So,* [7] ____________________, *Mom ...*

Amanda: [8] ____________________

We also might need to let the other person know that we didn't hear what they said:

Mom: [9] ____________________

Mom: [10] ____________________, *darling?*

Amanda: [11] ____________________

B Work in pairs. You are going to role-play a telephone conversation.

Student A – Call your partner to discuss one of the topics from the list below.

Student B – Listen to your partner. Make helpful suggestions before trying to bring the conversation to an end.

Then, swap roles.

- discuss a problem at work
- ask for a restaurant recommendation
- try to sell a new product
- ask to borrow some money

SPEAKING HUB

A **PREPARE** Work in pairs. Brainstorm the advantages and disadvantages of shared housing.

B **PLAN** Role-play a telephone conversation. Student A – Plan how to convince your partner not to move into a shared housing project. Student B – Plan how to convince your partner that moving into a shared housing project is a good idea.

C **SPEAK** Role-play the telephone call.

A: Yes, but if a lot of people are using the same facilities, they will break down sooner, so you might not be saving as much money as you think.

B: But houses are so expensive that we have to save money somehow.

Give your opinion on a social initiative

➤ Turn to page 160 to learn how to write a formal letter of complaint.

Unit 7 Review

VOCABULARY

A Choose the correct verbs to complete the sentences.

1 They plan to ***extend*** / ***construct*** the vacation resort by two square kilometers.
2 The local council are going to ***convert*** / ***relocate*** the hospital to a new site on the edge of town.
3 Almost all of the old factories in the city center have been ***restored*** / ***converted*** into apartments.
4 The old power station is going to be ***demolished*** / ***constructed*** to make way for a new shopping mall.
5 There are some beautiful old buildings in the city, but it would be expensive to ***restore*** / ***transform*** them.
6 After spending millions of dollars, the old docks have been ***transformed*** / ***extended*** into a vibrant area.
7 Plans to ***construct*** / ***relocate*** a new hospital have been put on hold due to financial constraints.

B Work in pairs. Discuss what changes you think should be made to your neighborhood and why.

C Match the numbers (1–8) with the letters (a–h) to form full sentences.

1 The city needs to come ...
2 New recycling bins have been installed in order to cut ...
3 The local government has teamed ...
4 While building the new road, the government ran ...
5 Facilities such as schools and hospitals can't keep ...
6 The country has spent a lot of money trying to catch ...
7 It's important to take care ...
8 I don't really get along ...

a up with local businesses to renovate the area.
b up with development in neighboring countries.
c of less fortunate people in society.
d up with a solution to the overcrowding.
e out of funding.
f up with the population growth in the area.
g with many of my neighbors.
h down on waste.

D Complete the compound nouns with the nouns in the box.

car food language street volunteer

1 A __________ party was organized to celebrate the royal wedding.
2 Since the introduction of a __________-sharing system, traffic levels have reduced almost by half.
3 For some people, access to a __________ bank is vital in order to feed their families.
4 I've really improved my level of English since I joined a __________ exchange.
5 After the floods, hundreds of __________ workers helped to clear up the area.

GRAMMAR

A Complete the first conditional sentences with the correct form of the verbs in the box.

call do finish reach sit work

1 If the city continues to grow, the population __________ ten million inhabitants soon.
2 If you get lost, __________ me.
3 What __________ if it rains?
4 If they meet the deadline, the new stadium __________ by the start of the season.
5 If you arrive late, we __________ on the beach.
6 You're not going to get promoted if you __________ harder.

B Choose the correct options to complete the sentences.

1 I wish you ***'d hurried up*** / ***'d hurry up***. We're going to be late.
2 If only we ***left*** / ***'d left*** earlier! I was so annoyed that we missed the beginning of the concert.
3 There's so much more I want to see here in Rome. If only we ***'d had*** / ***had*** more time.
4 I wish you ***could have come*** / ***could come***. It was so much fun.
5 I wish it ***hadn't rained*** / ***wasn't raining***. I'm so wet!
6 I wish my roommate ***would do*** / ***would have done*** the dishes more often. He never does it!
7 I think we're lost. If only I ***listened*** / ***'d listened*** to the directions more carefully.
8 If only I ***'d had*** / ***had*** more money. I definitely won't be going on vacation this year.

C What might you say in these situations? Write sentences with unreal conditional structures.

1 You would like to get a taxi but you have no reception on your phone.
____.
2 The map on your phone isn't working so you got lost.
____.
3 You would like to play soccer but your foot hurts.
____.
4 You should have started the essay sooner. You missed the deadline.
____.
5 I stayed out in the sun too long yesterday and got sunburned.
____.
6 Look at the weather in Lisbon this week! It's much better than last week when we were there.
____.

D Work in pairs. Compare your ideas from Exercise C.

8 MYSTERY

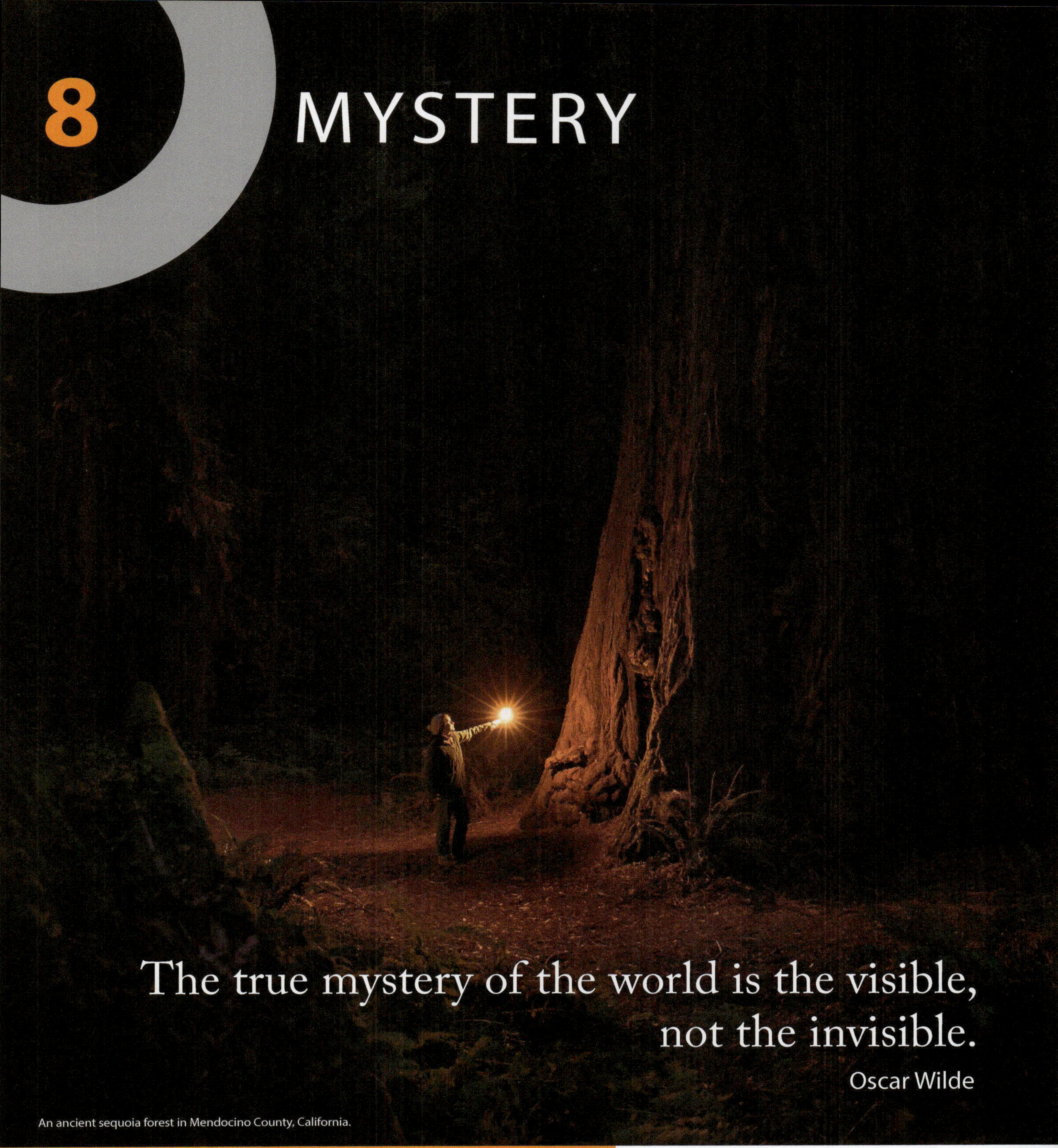

The true mystery of the world is the visible, not the invisible.

Oscar Wilde

An ancient sequoia forest in Mendocino County, California.

OBJECTIVES

- speculate about past events
- summarize a cultural story
- write and perform a short scene
- speculate about the causes and consequences of a crime
- discuss how to test an idea
- write a complex essay

Work with a partner. Discuss the questions.

1 Read the quote. What do you think Wilde means? Do you agree with him? Why/Why not?

2 What crime novels or TV shows do you enjoy watching? Tell your partner about one of them.

3 What crimes are the biggest problem in your society? What do you think can be done to deal with them?

8.1 Myths and legends

- Speculate about past events
- Summarize a cultural story

S – decoding: similes and metaphors
V – word families
G – past modals of deduction
P – thought groups

READING

A Do you believe that ghosts, aliens or monsters exist? How certain are you on a scale of 1–5 (1 = I'm sure they don't exist, 5 = I'm sure they do exist)? Write notes.

B **SPEAK** Work in groups. Compare your answers from Exercise A. Explain your ideas, giving examples where appropriate.

HOW DO YOU EXPLAIN THAT?

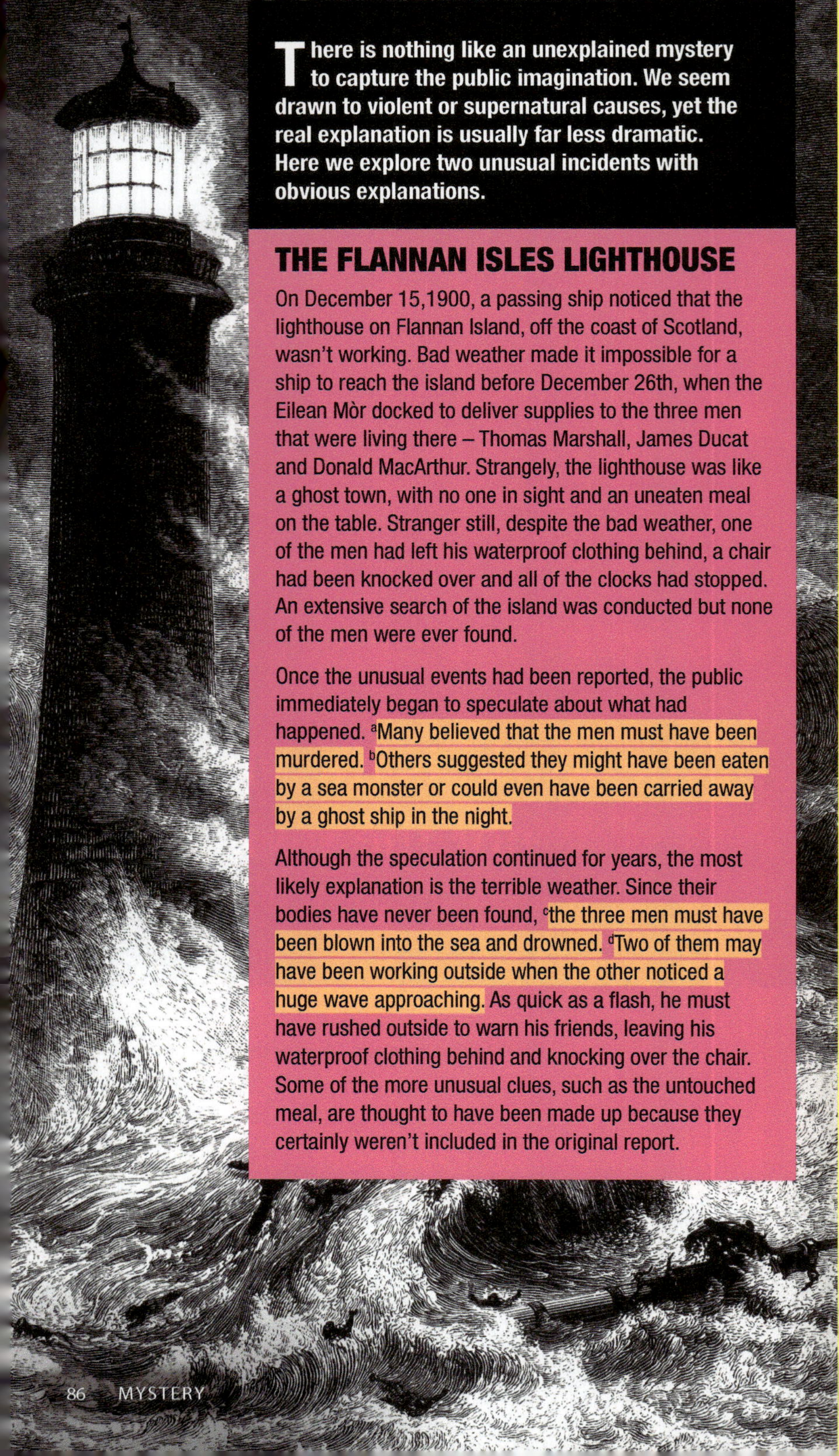

There is nothing like an unexplained mystery to capture the public imagination. We seem drawn to violent or supernatural causes, yet the real explanation is usually far less dramatic. Here we explore two unusual incidents with obvious explanations.

THE FLANNAN ISLES LIGHTHOUSE

On December 15,1900, a passing ship noticed that the lighthouse on Flannan Island, off the coast of Scotland, wasn't working. Bad weather made it impossible for a ship to reach the island before December 26th, when the Eilean Mòr docked to deliver supplies to the three men that were living there – Thomas Marshall, James Ducat and Donald MacArthur. Strangely, the lighthouse was like a ghost town, with no one in sight and an uneaten meal on the table. Stranger still, despite the bad weather, one of the men had left his waterproof clothing behind, a chair had been knocked over and all of the clocks had stopped. An extensive search of the island was conducted but none of the men were ever found.

Once the unusual events had been reported, the public immediately began to speculate about what had happened. [a]Many believed that the men must have been murdered. [b]Others suggested they might have been eaten by a sea monster or could even have been carried away by a ghost ship in the night.

Although the speculation continued for years, the most likely explanation is the terrible weather. Since their bodies have never been found, [c]the three men must have been blown into the sea and drowned. [d]Two of them may have been working outside when the other noticed a huge wave approaching. As quick as a flash, he must have rushed outside to warn his friends, leaving his waterproof clothing behind and knocking over the chair. Some of the more unusual clues, such as the untouched meal, are thought to have been made up because they certainly weren't included in the original report.

THE DYATLOV PASS INCIDENT

On February 2, 1959, nine hikers set out to climb Kholat Syakhl ('Mountain of the Dead') in Russia but never returned. Three weeks later, a search party found the group's badly damaged tent abandoned and half covered in snow. Footprints left by people who were either barefoot or wearing little on their feet led rescuers to the edge of a forest where they found five bodies, each with missing or ripped clothing. Although the hikers had sustained few external injuries, their skin had turned a strange shade of orange and investigators found high levels of radiation on their clothing. The other four bodies were found on May 4th, almost 100 meters away. Although better dressed than the first group, they had major injuries, including broken ribs and a fractured skull. Rescuers must have turned white as a sheet when they discovered that one of the female hikers was missing her tongue.

Theories of what had happened soon began to circulate. [e]Some thought the group might have been murdered by the indigenous Mansi people. Others suggested they had been attacked by wild animals or even a yeti. [f]However, the hikers can't have been murdered or attacked by animals because there were no signs of a fight. It is far more likely that the destruction of the tent and the second group's physical injuries were caused by an avalanche, while the missing tongue was probably eaten by a wild animal. The first group's lack of clothing can be explained by something called 'paradoxical undressing' – a phenomenon in which people in the final stages of hypothermia start to feel incredibly hot and take off their clothes in an attempt to cool down. Their orange skin and the radiation levels on their clothing are thought to have been caused by overexposure to the sun.

Glossary

avalanche (n) a large amount of snow and ice that suddenly falls down a mountain

C SCAN Scan *How do you explain that?* What explanations were originally given for each mystery?

D READ FOR DETAIL Read the stories again and answer the questions.

1 What had been left in the lighthouse?
2 What does the writer say happened to the men?
3 What does the writer think caused the chair to fall over?
4 Where were the two groups of bodies found?
5 What physical injuries had the hikers sustained?
6 What explanation is given for the missing tongue?

E DECODE: SIMILES AND METAPHORS Read the stories again. Answer the questions by identifying similes and metaphors in the text. Use the information in the box to help you.

Decoding: similes and metaphors

In articles describing dramatic events, writers frequently use descriptive language to make the story more engaging. Two common techniques used are:

a **Similes** – comparing one thing to another using *as* or *like*.
*He may look small, but he's **as brave as a lion**.*

b **Metaphors** – describing something as if it were something else.
*The snow **was a white blanket**. (= It wasn't actually a blanket; it just looked like one.)*

1 What was the lighthouse like when the ship arrived?
a like a small town b empty
2 How does the writer think the third man left the kitchen?
a slowly b quickly
3 How does the writer think the rescuers felt when they discovered the female hiker?
a frightened b angry

F SPEAK Work in groups. Why do you think people look for unusual explanations to mysteries, when there are frequently more obvious solutions?

GRAMMAR
Past modals of deduction

A Work in pairs. Look at the highlighted sentences in the article. Which sentence(s) mean …

1 it's almost certain that something happened or is true.
2 it's possible that something happened or is true.
3 it's impossible that something happened or is true.

B WORK IT OUT Complete the structures in the box.

Past modals of deduction

We use modals of deduction to make guesses about what happened in the past.

a We use ________ + *have* + past participle to say we're sure something happened because there's strong evidence.
b We use ________ / ________ / ________ + *have* + past participle to say we think something is possible, but we aren't sure.
c We use ________ + *have* + past participle to say we're sure something didn't happen because there's strong evidence.

C Work in pairs. Go to the Grammar Hub on page X.

D SPEAK Work in pairs. Read the situations (1–3) and discuss what you think happened using past modals of deduction.

1 Hundreds of children got sick at a school in New York. Children who brought in their own lunch were unaffected.
2 Tasmin took the train to work as normal and went to buy coffee from a café nearby. However, when she went to pay, she discovered her wallet was missing.
3 A math teacher was amazed when one of his students finished their exam in 20 minutes. The exam has 100 questions and usually takes an hour and a half.

SPEAKING

A DISCUSS Work in groups. Read *The Hopkinsville goblin case* and discuss what you think happened.

The Hopkinsville Goblin Case

In 1955, the Sutton family and their friend Billy Ray Taylor were relaxing on their porch. Suddenly, Billy Ray saw lights in the sky and shouted for everyone to come and take a look. They saw what they thought was an alien with glowing eyes, a large head, pointed ears and claws. The family and their friend grabbed their guns and started shooting. They heard their bullets hitting something metal, which they thought must have been the alien's spaceship.

B Go to the Communication Hub on page XXI and compare your ideas from Exercise A with the likely solution.

LISTENING

A SPEAK Work in pairs. Look at the illustrations of three famous myths from around the world. What do you think happens in each story? Where do you think these stories are from?

8.1 **B LISTEN FOR GIST** Listen to an interview with an expert on myths and legends. Check your ideas from Exercise A.

8.1 **C LISTEN FOR DETAIL** Listen again. Choose the correct options (a, b or c) to complete the sentences.

1 According to Phillip Norris, myths and legends …
   - a usually have the same origin.
   - b are similar in neighboring countries.
   - c have similar themes across cultures.

2 The tales of Sinbad the Sailor are given as an example of …
   - a a hero myth.
   - b a monster myth.
   - c an urban legend.

3 Sinbad and his crew go to the castle on the island …
   - a to look for food.
   - b to escape from their attackers.
   - c to shelter from the storm.

4 Anyone who looks directly at Medusa …
   - a is bitten by the snakes in her hair.
   - b is turned to stone.
   - c is killed by Perseus.

5 The Yeti and Bigfoot are given as examples of …
   - a stories inspired by wild animals.
   - b ancient legends.
   - c modern monster myths.

6 To call Hanako-San, you have to …
   - a knock on the bathroom mirror three times.
   - b say her name three times.
   - c knock on the bathroom door three times and say her name.

7 According to Phillip Norris, myths like Hanako-San are …
   - a unique to Japan.
   - b surprisingly different across cultures.
   - c popular with young children.

D SPEAK Work in groups. Why do you think myths and legends are still told today? Why do you think new ones are still created? Explain your reasoning.

VOCABULARY

Word families

A Complete the word families in the table. Use the information in the box to help you.

Word families

A word family is a group of words with the same root. Learning the associated words (e.g. the verb, noun, adjective and adverb) can help you to understand texts more easily and improve your accuracy when writing.

Verb	Noun	Adjective	Adverb
–	1	mythical	–
2	belief	3	believably
–	4	heroic	heroically
5	representation	representative	representatively
–	6	traditional	7
transform	8	transformational	–

B Complete the sentences with the correct form of the words in parentheses.

1 The minotaur is a ________________ (*myth*) creature with the head of a bull and the body of a man.

2 The main character usually ________________ (*hero*) saves a princess or someone else in distress.

3 Snakes are frequently used to ________________ (*represent*) danger.

4 ________________ (*tradition*), stories were told and not written down so there are frequently variations of a legend.

5 Many stories frequently include the ________________ (*transform*) of a person into some kind of monster.

PRONUNCIATION
Thought groups

8.2 **A** **Listen to the first part of a story from the interview. Mark any pauses with (/). Why do you think the speaker pauses at these points?**

As in many of the stories, Sinbad's ship is caught in a terrible storm and driven off course. They sail toward a small island but are attacked by a tribe of monkeys carrying spears. Fearing for their lives, Sinbad and his crew swim to the island and rush to a castle they see at the top of a hill.

8.3 **B** **Read the next part of the story. Mark where you think the speaker will pause with (/). Then listen and check.**

Tired and hungry from their escape, the crew falls asleep on the floor of the castle but is awoken to find the ground shaking. In the doorway to their room stands a giant over 20 meters tall. His eyes burn like fire, his teeth are long and sharp, and his huge mouth has the lips of a camel. Sinbad and his crew try to run away but one of them is caught and eaten by the giant.

C **SPEAK** **Work in pairs. Practice telling the story from Exercise B. Remember to use pauses to make the story easier to follow.**

SPEAKING HUB

A **PREPARE** Work in pairs. Look at the pictures and use the words in the box to discuss what you think each myth might be about.

Greeks hidden horse war

fake lake monster Scotland

accident coat forest hitchhiker

B **PLAN** Work in groups of three. Student A – Go to the Communication Hub on page XX. Student B – Go to the Communication Hub on page XXII. Student C – Go to the Communication Hub on page XIX.

C **PRESENT** Summarize the myth you have just read about to your group. Use your notes to help you.

D **DISCUSS** Work in pairs. Think about myths and legends in your own country. Tell your partner:

- who the myth was about
- what the origins of the myth were
- what happened in the myth

Speculate about past events
Summarize a cultural story

8.2 Who did it?

- Write and perform a short scene
- Speculate about the causes and consequences of a crime

V easily confused verbs; crime
S following an argument
G order of adjectives
P adding information

READING

A PREDICT Work in pairs. You are going to read part of a story called *The curse of the black falcon*. Look at the picture and discuss the questions.

1 What do you think the Black Falcon is?
2 What do you think happens in the story?

B SKIM Read the story quickly and check your predictions from Exercise A.

C READ FOR MAIN IDEA Read the story again. Are these sentences true (T) or false (F)? Correct the false sentences.

1 Professor Bainbridge was excited about having a party. T / F
2 Professor Bainbridge was most excited by the value of the necklace. T / F
3 He only got to keep the necklace for a short time. T / F
4 Only members of the family knew the code for the safe. T / F
5 The safe was hidden in the desk. T / F
6 The burglar broke the window immediately. T / F
7 The burglar searched the room calmly at first. T / F
8 A sudden noise alerted the professor to the burglar's presence. T / F

The Curse of the BLACK FALCON

'So, how do I look?'

Professor Bainbridge smiled as he turned to face his daughter. She was wearing a beautiful blue dress that had once belonged to his mother. Although Alice had recently turned 20, to him she'd always be the little girl who was too scared to sleep with the lights off. 'Like a million dollars,' he said, returning her smile.

Tonight was supposed to be a celebration, but he'd never liked parties, especially when he was the focus. He sighed, put his glasses down and rubbed his eyes. Seeing his reaction, Alice touched her father's arm and asked, 'Daddy, what's wrong? Aren't you excited to show everyone what you found?'

All of this fuss over an old necklace. True, it was worth a lot of money to the right collector, but to him its historical value was far more important. He'd heard stories about the mysterious Black Falcon all his life and after years of research and hard work, he'd finally found it in a muddy French field. It was such a significant find that his family had insisted that they hold a party to celebrate. On Monday, the professor would deliver the necklace to the British Museum, but for the weekend it would stay locked away in the safe above his desk. Nobody outside of the family knew the combination to the safe, but it still made him nervous to have such a valuable object in his house. He looked up at the large rectangular painting above the desk, tried to straighten it and turned back to his daughter.

'I'll be happier when this weekend is over,' he said angrily. Recognizing that her father was nervous, Alice began to straighten his bow tie. 'You never know, you might have fun.' The professor was just about to reply when the doorbell rang. 'That'll be the Joneses!' Alice said excitedly. 'They're always early. Come on!' The professor sighed again and followed her out into the hallway.

For an hour, the study lay empty. The fire had died out and the only sound came from the antique gold clock on the desk and the thunderstorm outside. Suddenly, a figure dressed in black appeared at the window. Cautiously, they looked into the study. Satisfied that the room was empty, they raised a fist to the window. Yet, instead of breaking the glass immediately, they stopped. For two long minutes they waited, patiently watching the sky until suddenly, the moment came. A loud crash of thunder echoed through the sky and the figure calmly smashed the window, felt for the handle and climbed inside.

Slowly, they began opening drawers and pulling books off the shelves, but as the minutes ticked by, they became more and more desperate. Frustrated, the figure leaned against the desk and stared at the painting above it. Noticing it was hanging at a strange angle, the figure moved the painting to the side, revealing the strong metal safe behind. After a few minutes, the safe was open and inside lay the ultimate prize – the Black Falcon.

Just as the figure reached inside to grab the necklace, they heard the professor's voice ringing through the hallway outside. 'I'll just go and fetch my pipe … See you outside.' In their hurry to find somewhere to hide, the figure sent a small Chinese vase crashing to the ground. Terrified, the figure hid behind the open door, holding the necklace as the professor appeared on the other side. 'Tommy? Is that you?' he called, looking into the darkness. He listened for a reply but there was nothing but silence.

D INFER MEANING **Work in pairs. Scan the story again and discuss the questions.**

1 What does the professor mean when he says that Alice looks 'like a million dollars'?
2 Why does the figure in black wait before breaking the window?
3 How does the burglar work out where the Black Falcon is?

VOCABULARY
Easily confused verbs

A Choose the correct options to complete the sentences. Then scan the story again to check your answers.

1 ***Seeing / Watching*** his reaction, Alice ***felt / touched*** her father's arm and asked …
2 For two long minutes they waited, patiently ***watching / seeing*** the sky until suddenly, …
3 … the figure calmly smashed the window, ***touched / felt*** for the handle and climbed inside.
4 … they ***heard / listened*** the professor's voice ringing through the hallway outside.
5 'Tommy? Is that you?' he called, ***seeing / looking*** into the darkness.
6 He ***listened / heard*** for a reply but there was nothing but silence.

B Complete the sentences with the correct form of the words in Exercise A.

1 Standing inside the room, he ________________ carefully to what they were saying outside.
2 He ________________ along the wall until he found the light switch.
3 He sat ________________ them to see what they would do.
4 ________________ the news, she rushed quickly to tell the others.
5 He ________________ in the direction of the safe and saw that the picture had been moved.
6 As he entered the room, he ________________ that the window had been smashed.
7 He carefully ________________ the necklace before picking it up.
8 ________________ a noise upstairs, she put down her broom and went to investigate.

C Work in pairs. Discuss the questions.

1 What's the most interesting piece of news you've heard this week?
2 Do you prefer to watch movies at the movie theater or stream them online? Why?
3 Do you think you could find your way around your home by touch alone?
4 Do you think listening to other people's conversations is a good way to learn English? Why/Why not?
5 What's the worst movie you've ever seen? Why was it so bad?

GRAMMAR
Order of adjectives

A Scan the story again. Underline sentences in which two or more adjectives are used to describe a noun.

B WORK IT OUT **Choose the correct options to complete the rules. Use the sentences in Exercise A to help you.**

> **Order of adjectives**
>
> When we use two or more adjectives to describe a noun, we usually put the adjectives in [1]***alphabetical order / a specific order***.
>
> Opinion adjectives (e.g. *amazing, incredible*) are always used [2]***before / after*** descriptive adjectives (e.g. *ancient, leather*).

C **Go to the Grammar Hub on page X.**

D PRACTICE **Rewrite the sentences using the adjectives in parentheses.**

1 He drives a car. (*expensive / old*)
____.
2 They walked slowly through the woods. (*dark / quiet*)
____.
3 She opened the door. (*wooden / noisy*)
____.
4 She had a bag. (*leather / red*)
____.
5 She was wearing shoes. (*Italian / beautiful*)
____.
6 In the living room, there was a table. (*wooden / antique / stunning*)
____.
7 The house was surrounded by trees. (*old / tall*)
____.
8 In the garden, there was a statue. (*stone / ancient*)
____.

E SPEAK **Student A – Go to the Communication Hub on page XXII. Student B – Go to the Communication Hub on page XIX.**

SPEAKING

A PREPARE **You are going to write and perform the next scene from *The curse of the black falcon*. With a partner, discuss what might happen next. Does the burglar escape or are they caught by the professor? Write notes about the key events in your scene.**

B PLAN **Write a conversation with one of you as the burglar and the other as the professor. Practice acting it out.**

C SPEAK **Perform your scene for the class. Vote on which pair has the best ending.**

VOCABULARY
Crime

A **Work in groups. Look at the pictures and discuss the questions.**

1 What do the pictures show? What's the connection between them?

2 Which do you think is more reliable? Why?

B **Complete the definitions with the correct form of the words in bold.**

1 There was a **burglary** here last night. The thieves took money, jewelry and electronic goods.

2 He tried to **bribe** the police with $5,000 to let him go.

3 I was a victim of **identity theft** when someone hacked into my computer and stole my bank details.

4 During the **robbery,** they threatened the sales clerk with a knife.

5 I was the victim of **fraud** when someone tricked me into giving them my bank details. They took $2,000.

6 I was **blackmailed** into helping the criminal gang to break into our offices.

a ________________ (v) to make someone give you money or do what you want by threatening to reveal compromising information about them

b ________________ (n) when someone illegally enters a building and steals things

c ________________ (n) the crime of obtaining money from someone by tricking them

d ________________ (v) to give money or presents to someone so that they will help you

e ________________ (n) the crime of taking money or property illegally by using threats or violence

f ________________ (n) the illegal use of somebody else's name and personal information to obtain goods, credit cards, etc.

C Go to the **Vocabulary Hub** on **page XVII**.

1

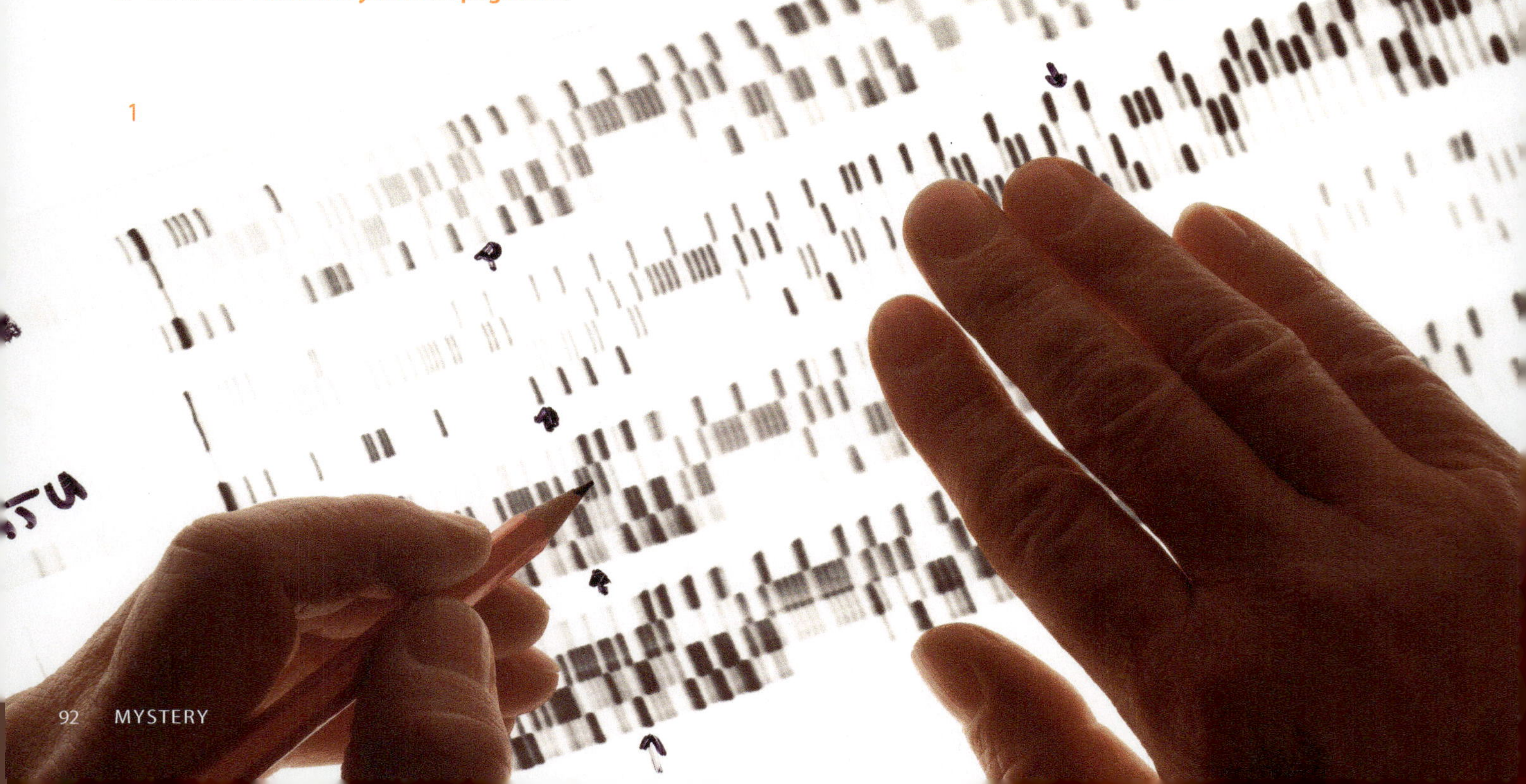

D **SPEAK** **Work in pairs. What do you think is the most effective way to catch the criminal in each example? Think about:**

- CCTV
- digital footprints
- DNA
- eyewitnesses
- phone histories
- fingerprints

LISTENING

A **SPEAK** **Work in pairs. Tell your partner about something interesting, unusual or frightening that has happened to you. Then discuss the questions.**

1 How accurate do you think this memory is?

2 Think about other people there at the time. Would their memory of the event be the same?

8.4 **B** **LISTEN FOR ORGANIZATION** **Listen to a talk about memory and eyewitness testimony. Put the topics in the order they are discussed.**

___ using language to influence memory

___ creating false memories

___ how the human memory works

___ the impact on the real world

___ blocking out painful memories

8.5 **C** **LISTEN FOR CONCLUSIONS** **Work in pairs. Listen to the last part of the talk again. What conclusion does the speaker make about eyewitness testimonies?**

D FOLLOW AN ARGUMENT **Listen to the full talk again. Complete the summary of each section with no more than three words from the talk. Use the information in the box to help you.**

8.4

> **Following an argument**
>
> In talks, speakers usually build to one clear conclusion. To reach this point, they use each section of the talk to develop their argument. To help you follow an argument, listen for when the speaker:
>
> - asks a question, then answers it – this helps them highlight the main ideas
> - uses pronoun referencing – this helps them refer back to the main ideas
> - gives a definition – this allows them to use key vocabulary

1 Our memories are unreliable because we rewrite or add to them each time we ____________________.

2 Although the idea of repressed memories was popular in the 1980s, studies since strongly indicate that patients were encouraged to create false memories by their ____________________.

3 The 1974 Loftus study showed that the way you ____________________ or talk about an event can influence someone's memory of it.

4 To many, studies like this explained how patients in the 1980s might have been encouraged to ____________________ their own childhood memories.

5 The 1995 Loftus study demonstrated that people can actually be convinced to create ____________________ childhood memories.

E SPEAK **Work in pairs and follow these instructions:**

Student A – Turn to **page 97**. Look at the picture for 30 seconds. Close your book. Tell Student B as much that you can remember about the picture as possible.

Student B – Turn to **page 97**. Look at the picture and listen to your partner's description. How accurate is their memory?

F **Now change roles using the image on page 109.**

PRONUNCIATION

Adding information

A **Listen to an extract from the lecture. Is the phrase in bold said with a falling tone (↘), rising tone (↗) or fall-rising tone (↘↗)?**

8.6

The information presented by a witness may have been influenced by the way in which they were questioned after the event. **On top of that**, lawyers could encourage witnesses to add or change details.

B **Work in pairs. What is the function of the phrase in Exercise A?**

a to change the topic

b to give an explanation

c to add information

C **Listen and repeat the sentences.**

8.7

1 Sounds ridiculous, doesn't it? **But actually**, the way we question someone can have a dramatic effect on how they describe what happened.

2 Juries are asked to pay close attention to eyewitness testimonies, but they are arguably not a reliable source. **Furthermore**, they can be affected by the stress and anxiety of, for instance, a violent robbery.

SPEAKING HUB

A PLAN **Read the situation and write notes about the victim, crime and any other important details.**

On Saturday, December 23, the billionaire oil tycoon Magnus Baldursson held a dinner party at his house to celebrate his retirement. At around 10:00 pm, his daughter's body was found at the bottom of the main staircase with a broken neck. She's thought to have been murdered.

B PREPARE **Work in groups. Turn to page XVIII.**

C DISCUSS **In your groups, discuss who you think killed Sophia and why.**

A: It must have been Albert. He said he is happy that Sofia's dead!

B: Yes, but he has an alibi. He was eating dinner in the kitchen.

– Write and perform a short scene

– Speculate about the causes and consequences of a crime

8.3 Fact or fiction?

A – understatement   S – maintaining a conversation

An urban legend

COMPREHENSION

A **Work in groups. Which of the following do you think are true and which are urban legends?**

1. If you drop a penny from the top of a skyscraper it will kill anyone it lands on.
2. Sharks can detect a single drop of blood from the other end of a swimming pool.
3. Using your cell phone at a gas station could trigger an explosion.

Glossary

crane (n) a tall machine with a long arm used for lifting and moving heavy objects
dummy (n) a model of a person, typically used for displaying clothes in a store window
Portaloo™ (n) a temporary toilet inside a small building that can be easily moved from place to place

B **Watch a segment from a TV show about urban legends and answer the questions.**

1. Which urban legend is discussed in the video?
2. How does the presenter and his team test the legend?
3. What is the conclusion of the experiment?

C **Watch again. Complete the sentences with no more than three words from the segment.**

1. The team dropped the Portaloo™ from a height of ____________ onto a concrete surface.
2. The first test showed that doing ____________ would result in serious injury.
3. The slow-motion video shows that the ____________ impact travels upward through the body.
4. For the second test, the team makes the ____________ body-double 'jump' before impact.
5. The second test showed it isn't possible to jump upward quick enough to make a real difference to the speed that ____________.

AUTHENTIC ENGLISH

A 00:47–01:12 **Watch part of the video again. Do the reactions of the presenter and his colleague make the situation sound more or less serious than it is?**

B **Match the situations (1–5) with their understated descriptions (a–e). Use the information in the box to help you.**

Understatement

An understatement is a sentence that makes a situation seem less important, serious, big, etc than it really is.

Two ways to make an understatement are by:

1. **modifying the noun**
   *OK, so we have **a little** problem with the car – it's been stolen.*
   *I'm afraid there's **a slight** issue with your card, sir. The payment has been declined.*
2. **rephrasing the sentence**
   You've put me in a terrible position. → *This is not the best position to be in.*
   I can't remember the last time I felt this bad! → *Well, I've definitely felt worse.*

1. You accidentally deleted an important document.
2. You almost died in a car crash.
3. Your house was robbed and everything was stolen.
4. It's minus thirty degrees outside.
5. You're so sick that you can't get out of bed.

a 'It's a little bit cold outside.'
b 'Yeah, it was pretty scary I guess.'
c 'So, I'm not really feeling 100% to be honest.'
d 'OK, don't worry, but there's been a little incident at home.'
e 'Uh, there's a slight issue with the report.'

C **Work in pairs. Take turns describing an extreme situation, then giving an understated description of it.**

A: You broke your leg in a climbing accident!
B: Yes, it was kind of painful …

Don't believe everything you hear

A Work in pairs. Imagine that you are trapped in a room. What different methods might you use to try to escape?

B Watch the video and answer the questions.

1 Which of your ideas from Exercise A do Harry and Sam try?
2 Where are they getting their ideas from?
3 How do they eventually escape?

SPEAKING SKILL

A Work in pairs. Read the extract from the conversation and discuss the questions.

1 What is the function of the highlighted phrase?
2 Why is it appropriate in this situation?
3 What other phrases could you use?

Sam: What now?
Harry: OK. We'll just have to call someone and get them to open the door from the other side using the spare key. Does that sound like a plan?

B Watch the video again. Complete the box with examples from the conversation.

Maintaining a conversation

When we are working together to solve a problem, we frequently keep the discussion going by asking others what they think of our suggestions. To do this, we use phrases such as:

Does that sound like a plan?, ________________, ________________, ________________, ________________.

C Read the situation below and brainstorm possible solutions.

You are driving through the countryside at night when suddenly your car breaks down. There's no cell phone signal and you didn't pass any houses or other buildings for miles before you broke down. There are no streetlights and very little moonlight.

D Work in groups. Discuss your ideas from Exercise C and try to agree on one solution. Use phrases from the box to maintain the conversation.

SPEAKING HUB

A PLAN Look back at the urban legends at the beginning of the lesson. Brainstorm different ways to effectively test each legend.

B PREPARE Choose your best suggestion for each test in Exercise A. Write notes about:

- what equipment you would need
- why this is an effective test
- how many times you would run the test and why
- any potential issues

C SPEAK Work in groups. Discuss your ideas from Exercise B and try to agree on one test for each urban legend.

Well, we can't really drop a coin from a skyscraper onto someone's head! I mean, I think that would hurt a little!

D PRESENT Present your ideas to the class and answer any questions.

Discuss how to test an idea

➤ Turn to page XXV to learn how to write a complex essay.

Unit 8 Review

VOCABULARY

A Complete the text with the correct form of the words in bold.

The Kitsune is a [1] __________ Japanese creature.	**MYTH**
It has the ability to [2] __________ from a fox into a human, but it does not look like a normal fox.	**TRANSFORM**
In [3] __________ stories, the Kitsune could fly, become invisible and produce fire and lightning. People had the	**TRADITION**
[4] __________ that as the creature got older, it became stronger and more intelligent. Once it reached one hundred, the creature could take a form that	**BELIEVE**
[5] __________ a human. It could also enter people's dreams and drive them mad. In many ways, the creature is similar to the	**REPRESENT**
[6] __________ characters in Pokémon, but the Kitsune was much more evil and considered a great trickster.	**HERO**

B Complete the sentences with the correct form of the words from the box.

feel hear listen look see touch watch

1 The fog was so thick we couldn't __________ where we were going.
2 He hid behind the door, __________ as they argued about what to do.
3 They suddenly woke up. 'Did you __________ that noise?' she asked.
4 She reached out and gently __________ his hand.
5 They __________ in horror as the cars crashed into each other.
6 __________ closely, he noticed that some of the things on his desk had been moved.
7 They could __________ the cold draft coming through the door.

C Choose the correct options (a, b or c) to complete the sentences.

1 At the courthouse last night, Mr. Taylor was ___ to 15 years in prison.
a committed b charged c sentenced
2 He admitted to using sensitive information to ___ the former star.
a blackmail b bribe c charge
3 Police have released footage of the armed ___ at the gas station.
a robbery b burglary c identity theft
4 Mr. Baxter says he ___ for five hours without a break.
a was charged b was arrested c was questioned
5 The men are accused of ___ multiple crimes in the area.
a witnessing b committing c investigating

D Work in pairs. Discuss the questions.

1 What do you think is the most common crime in your country?
2 What could be done to address crime in your city?
3 How can you protect yourself against identity theft?

GRAMMAR

A Rewrite the underlined sentences with *must* / *might* / *can't* + *have* + past participle.

1 They should be here by now. Maybe they got lost on the way.
They __________
__________.
2 I'm sure it wasn't Erin you saw last night. She's in Madrid.
You __________
__________.
3 I'm sure Max got the promotion. He was looking very happy earlier!
Max __________
__________.
4 I was cleaning up earlier. It's possible I threw the letter away by accident.
I __________
__________.
5 I'm sure I didn't leave my phone at work. I had it on the train.
I __________
__________.
6 Oh, no! I'm sure you booked the wrong tickets by mistake!
You __________
__________.

B Work in pairs. Take turns reading the sentences below, then responding with a modal of deduction.

1 Where's Emily? She should be here by now.
2 Did you hear that weird noise this morning?
3 So I saw your best friend outside earlier.

C Choose the correct options to complete the sentences.

1 He collects *Japanese antique* / *antique Japanese* vases.
2 They found some ***ancient gold*** / ***gold ancient*** coins in the field.
3 We're staying in a ***wonderful little*** / ***little wonderful*** town on the coast.
4 The town is full of ***amazing French*** / ***French amazing*** architecture.
5 They've rented a ***luxury huge*** / ***huge luxury*** villa for their vacation.
6 It's a ***beautiful 19th century*** / ***19th century beautiful*** mirror.
7 The ***valuable Russian gold*** / ***valuable gold Russian*** egg sold for millions.
8 He wore a ***new blue*** / ***blue new*** shirt for their date.

9 BUSINESS

The highest use of capital is not to make more money, but make money do more for the betterment of life.

Henry Ford

A Vietnamese entrepreneur transports her products in Haiphong, Vietnam.

OBJECTIVES

- talk about the risks and benefits of apps
- make an effective complaint about a product or service
- conduct a survey about what influences our purchases
- design and present an ad campaign
- discuss investment opportunities
- write a proposal

Work with a partner. Discuss the questions.

1 Read the quote. What roles in society do you think businesses have other than making money?

2 Do you think the future belongs to big businesses or to start-up companies and entrepreneurs? Explain your reasoning.

3 When looking for a new job are you more attracted to a high salary or challenging work? Why?

9.1 Customers

- Talk about the risks and benefits of apps
- Make an effective complaint about a product or service

G – adjective clauses
S – fronting
P – pitch on non-essential adjective clauses
V – dependent prepositions: verbs

READING

A SPEAK Work in groups. Would you trust a stranger to do the following? Why/Why not?

- drive you somewhere
- stay at your house
- recommend something
- give you advice
- rate your skills
- judge your interactions

B READ FOR MAIN IDEA Read *Who would you trust?* Complete the article with the headings below.

- affecting your career
- new technology, new economy
- the influence of the consumer
- the benefits of and need for reviews
- the future of ratings

Who would *you* trust?

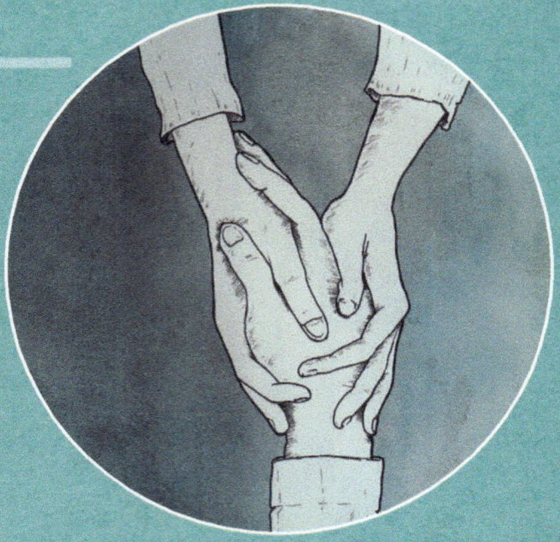

[1]Who are the people in your life that you place your trust in? What does someone have to do to earn your trust? In today's technology-driven world, it seems we are more willing than ever to trust the word of complete strangers.

By Leonard Jackson | July 16, 2018

a ______________________

Trust has always played an essential role in the economy. [2]In the past, we placed our trust in our neighbors – people in our local community that had developed a good reputation for the products and services they offered. As major cities grew, we came to trust the reputation of companies and institutions. Individuals could start businesses, but it took time for them to establish a good reputation. Technology, and the way that it has enabled individuals to set up businesses and allowed others to rate them, has changed all of this. Just a few years ago, neither of the online services Uber or Airbnb existed, but both are now hugely popular. [3]Thanks to Uber, which lets people use an app to order a ride at a generally much lower rate than a normal taxi firm, we are all potential taxi drivers. And the website Airbnb, which lets you stay in other people's houses or apartments, means that a spare bedroom in your house is a money-making opportunity.

b ______________________

Star-rating systems have been around for decades on Amazon and eBay, but mobile technology has made them much more accessible. Online shopping, which is clearly quicker and more efficient than regular shopping, doesn't allow us to physically try out the products. Ratings have helped to fill this gap. Consumers also tend to be good judges of how authentic a review is. For example, a product that doesn't have any negative reviews is likely to be viewed with some suspicion. Allowing customers to see both the good and bad in a product usually means they trust the reviews more – much more than something that constantly gets five stars.

c ______________________

Mobile technology has given people much more power to influence the reputation of a company. When Kylie Jenner sent a negative tweet about Snapchat, the company's value fell by over $1 billion in one day. [4]Of course, we don't all have the influence of famous celebrities, but companies now hire people whose job is to monitor mentions of their brands so they can provide instant customer support. Those companies that fail to react quickly run the risk of negative opinions and experiences going viral. In the past, complaining may have involved going into a store or writing a series of letters, but now good companies respond in minutes.

d ______________________

Our own online reputation can also have a significant effect on our real-world prospects. [5]Recruiters now regularly check out people's online profiles before interviewing or hiring them and the first thing they see are social media profiles. LinkedIn – the professional networking site – can have a huge influence on people's careers. In the past, employers posted job ads online hoping to attract the best talent; now they actively seek out prospective employees via endorsements on LinkedIn. Companies trust the accuracy of these online reviews of our experience and abilities even though they may have never met the people that wrote them.

e ______________________

So, how might our reputation be measured in the future? [6]Well, it's not difficult to imagine a world where our every interaction affects a social credit score. What we share or buy online, the content we 'like', even the people we connect with could all contribute to an overall rating that affects what we're able to do in the real world. Although this may sound like science fiction, a future in which we are rated on everything may not be that unrealistic.

C READ FOR DETAIL Read again. Complete the sentences with no more than two words from the article.

1 New technology has allowed customers to ________________ new businesses.
2 A rating system can reduce the ________________ between customers and sellers.
3 People are unlikely to trust a product with no ________________.
4 Customers can now ________________ what a company does.
5 Businesses employ people to monitor ________________ of their company online so that they can deal with issues quickly.
6 Our own personal online ________________ could affect our future job prospects.
7 Companies look for ________________ using networking sites like LinkedIn.
8 The writer believes that in the future we may use a ________________ based on how we interact online.

D SPEAK Work in groups. Discuss the questions.

1 Do you usually check online reviews before buying or doing something? Why/Why not?
2 Have you ever complained about a product or service via social media?
3 What can you do to protect or improve your online reputation?

GRAMMAR
Adjective clauses

A Look at the highlighted sentences in the article. Underline the adjective clauses in each.

B SPEAK Work in pairs. Are the clauses you underlined in Exercise A essential or non-essential? How do you know?

C WORK IT OUT Match the sentences (1–6) from Exercise A to the rules (a–f).

Adjective clauses

In essential adjective clauses:
- we can use *that* instead of *who* or *which* [a] ___
- we can omit the relative pronoun when it's the object of the adjective clause [b] ___

In non-essential adjective clauses:
- we use commas to separate the clause from the rest of the sentence [c] ___

In both types of adjective clause:
- we use *where* to talk about places [d] ___ and *whose* to talk about possession [e] ___ – neither of which can be omitted
- we use prepositions at the beginning of a clause in formal English and at the end in informal English [f] ___

D Go to the **Grammar Hub** on **page XII**.

E SPEAK Work in groups. Try to improve the following review using adjective clauses like the one in the example.

Apps Games Reviews

★★★★☆

Meal Maker
is a great app!

ClaireP | 2 days ago

This is the best app *that I've ever downloaded!* It has a lot of useful features including a meal tracker. I also like the recipes. Another good feature is the fitness section. There's also a community space. I was actually sent a recipe by an old friend! Anyway, I'd definitely recommend this app.

PRONUNCIATION
Pitch on non-essential adjective clauses

A 9.1 **Listen to this extract from a radio show about apps. Does the speaker's pitch step up or down on the non-essential adjective clause?**

Trello, which I use to stay organized at work, is the most useful app on my phone.

B 9.2 **Listen and repeat the sentences.**

1 MyFitnessPal, which records daily food and exercise, is a good app for helping you lose weight.
2 Spotify, which allows you to stream music offline, is something I use every day.
3 Mint, which links all your bank cards, is a great app for keeping track of your finances.

SPEAKING

A PLAN Make a list of apps that you use regularly on your phone or tablet.

B PRESENT Work in pairs. Compare your lists from Exercise A. Explain any apps that your partner doesn't know or use.

A: I've heard of most of these, but what's Strava?
B: Uh, It's a fitness app that tracks how far you run.

C DISCUSS Work in pairs. Rank the apps in Exercise B from most to least useful. Then discuss any risks involved with each and how they might be improved.

LISTENING

A SPEAK Complete *Are you a good complainer?* Compare your answers with a partner. Give reasons for your approach.

B Go to the **Communication Hub** on **page XXI** to find out what type of complainer you are.

9.3 **C LISTEN FOR GIST** Listen to a customer make a complaint about something they ordered online. Answer the questions.

1. What does the customer want to complain about?
2. What two solutions does the customer service representative offer?
3. Is the customer happy with these solutions? Why/Why not?
4. Why can't the customer service representative resolve the issue now?

9.3 **D LISTEN FOR FRONTING** Listen again. Choose the correct options (a, b or c) to complete the sentences. Use the information in the box to help you.

Fronting

In informal spoken English, speakers sometimes move part of a clause from its normal position to the beginning of a sentence.

How you thought you'd get away with it, I'll never know.

Never have I been so disappointed.

This non-standard word order is called fronting and is used for emphasis or dramatic effect.

1. The customer had to wait for ___ to speak to a customer service representative.
   a two minutes
   b five minutes
   c 40 minutes
2. The customer doesn't think the delivery should have been left ___
   a in the backyard.
   b under the patio table.
   c in the children's playhouse.
3. The customer expects the company to ___
   a issue a full refund for the damaged books.
   b offer a discount on his next purchase.
   c replace the most damaged books.
4. The customer paid ___ for the books.
   a $10
   b $150
   c $100
5. The customer thinks ___ is ridiculous.
   a the customer service representative
   b the company's terms of service
   c the company's refunds and exchange policy

E SPEAK In some cultures, people prefer not to complain directly. How common is it to complain in your culture? How do you think people react to bad service or faulty products?

Are you a good complainer?

In some countries, complaining could almost be a national sport. In others, people rarely complain about anything. To find out what type of complainer you are, decide what you would do in the following situations.

1 You order some books from a well-known online retailer, but when they arrive most of them are damaged.
a Say nothing and keep the books. It's still possible to read them; they just don't look very nice.
b Share the story on social media, swearing to never use the company again.
c Contact the company directly and ask for a refund or a replacement.

2 You order a cup of coffee at a well-known chain, but when it arrives it's the wrong drink.
a Drink it anyway. It might not be what you ordered, but it's still delicious.
b Post a comment publicly shaming the company on their social media page.
c Politely point out the mistake to staff and ask for a new drink.

3 You accidentally sit in the first class section of train and are caught by the ticket inspector.
a Pay the fine. You made a mistake, so you should face the consequences.
b Refuse to pay and post a video of the argument that follows on social media.
c Accept responsibility, but send an email to the train company suggesting they use clearer signs in first class.

4 You order a tuna sandwich from Andy's Café, but ask them to remove the cucumber because you don't like it. When you take your first bite, you realize they haven't done what you asked.
a Remove the cucumber yourself and eat the sandwich anyway.
b Share a picture of the sandwich online with the hashtag '#avoidandyscafe'
c Politely explain the issue to staff and ask for a new sandwich.

5 You oversleep on a business trip and miss an early morning flight. The airline company won't let you on the next flight without a new ticket.
a Buy a new ticket. It's your fault that you missed the flight.
b Post a video of your argument with the airline company on social media.
c Accept responsibility, but email the airline company suggesting they offer more support to customers in your situation.

VOCABULARY

Dependent prepositions: verbs

Dependent prepositions: verbs

Some verbs and prepositions are commonly used together. These are called dependent prepositions and they are followed by either a noun or *-ing*.
For example:
How do you intend to deal with this issue? NOT ~~*How do you intend to deal about this issue?*~~

9.4 **A Complete the extracts from the phone call with the prepositions in the box. Then listen and check.**

about (x2) for (x2) on to (x2) with

1 Thank you _________ holding; we appreciate your call.
2 I'm calling to complain _________ the condition of the books I received.
3 I understand that, but at no point did I consent _________ the books being left somewhere they could get damaged!
4 I understand that, but I really must insist _________ a full refund.
5 I'm afraid that since we have adhered _________ your delivery instructions, the most I'd be able to offer is $10 off your next purchase.
6 Look, I don't want to argue _________ this anymore!
7 24 hours? Why can't this be dealt _________ right now?
8 I can only apologize _________ any inconvenience caused.

B Are these sentences correct or incorrect? Rewrite the incorrect sentences.

1 Cheap Flights would like to apologize for any inconvenience caused by this delay.
2 You should have complained at having to wait so long to be served.
3 I'm sick of being passed between different people – I just want someone to deal with this issue!
4 I realize you've adhered in company policy, but I'm still not satisfied.
5 Gary, can you help me? There's a customer downstairs who keeps insisting at speaking to the manager.
6 Look, we've been arguing on this for the past 45 minutes. Either issue a refund or let me speak to your manager.
7 When you completed the purchase online, you consented with our terms and conditions.
8 Let me take this opportunity to thank all of you for giving us your feedback today.

SPEAKING HUB

A PLAN Work in pairs. Think of phrases you could use to complain about a product and how you could respond to these complaints.

B SPEAK Student A – Imagine you are a customer service representative. Use the stages below to help you resolve your partner's complaint. Student B – Imagine you are a customer. Go to the Communication Hub on page XXII.

1 Find out how you can help the customer.
2 Find out if the product is broken.
3 Ask if something else could be causing the fault, e.g. the internet provider.
4 Check if the product is still under warranty.
5 Suggest sending someone out to repair the product.
6 Tell the customer that exchanges are not part of the company policy.
7 Tell the customer you will refer the complaint to your supervisor.

**C REPEAT Change roles. Student A – Go to the Communication Hub on page XX.
Student B – Use the stages in Exercise B to help you resolve your partner's complaint.**

D DISCUSS Who had the most successful complaint? Tell the class and give reasons.

- Talk about the risks and benefits of apps
- Make an effective complaint about a product or service

9.2 Products

- Conduct a survey about what influences our purchases
- Design and present an ad campaign

V – science; advertising
P – connected speech: determiners and quantifiers
G – determiners and quantifiers
S – topic sentences

VOCABULARY

Science

A Read *The book club*. Complete the definitions with the words in bold.

1 ________________ (n) a process of studying or examining something in order to understand or explain it
2 ________________ (n) people who study something carefully to discover new information about it
3 ________________ (n) one or more ideas that explain how or why something happens
4 ________________ (n) facts or signs that make you believe something is true
5 ________________ (n) facts or information used for making calculations or decisions

B Complete the sentences with words from Exercise A.

1 The company has collected ________________ from over 20,000 people worldwide.
2 ________________ claim the results indicate a clear link between stress and high blood pressure.
3 I'm sorry, but there simply isn't enough ________________ to support that claim.
4 ________________ of the data showed a link between the consumption of fish and improved memory.
5 One ________________ is that consumers don't actually question the claims made in advertising.

LISTENING

A SPEAK Work in pairs. Do you think the following sentences are facts (F) or myths (M)? Explain your reasoning.

1 We should drink eight glasses of water a day. ___
2 Eggs are bad for your heart. ___
3 Yogurt is good for digestion. ___
4 Eat less food when you have a fever. ___
5 Eating cheese can give you nightmares. ___
6 Natural sugar is better for us than processed sugar. ___

9.5 **B LISTEN FOR MAIN IDEA** Listen to a radio interview about health myths. According to the scientist, which three of the claims in Exercise A are myths?

Glossary

dehydration (n) a dangerous lack of water in the body

The Book Club

Episode 402: Science fact or fiction?

According to **researchers** from the McCallun Institute, over 80% of Americans still believe that Vitamin C cures the common cold, despite the fact that there is little to no **evidence** to support this **theory**. In her new book, *Science fact or fiction?*, Professor Dawn Jackson uses her **analysis** of hundreds of consumer studies to argue that believing in health myths may actually affect the products we buy. She goes on to claim that companies take advantage of this fact in their marketing campaigns. But are Jackson's observations really supported by the research **data**? Michael Evans spoke to her earlier this week to find out.

9.5 **C LISTEN FOR DETAIL** Listen again. Complete the sentences with no more than three words or a number from the podcast.

1 According to the professor, the ________________ benefits from the commonly held belief that we need to drink eight glasses of water a day.
2 There's no evidence that increasing your intake of ________________ will help the body fight infections such as the common cold.
3 The professor argues that we can only be confident of a health claim if there is a large body of ________________ to support it.
4 Probiotics, also known as '________________ bacteria', are generally thought to be beneficial to the digestive system.
5 Companies need to be careful about ________________ ________________ used in advertising as they cannot legally make claims that aren't supported by evidence.
6 While ________________ are associated with a number of negative health effects, the professor says we don't need to worry about how much fruit we consume.

D SPEAK Work in pairs. Why do you think so many companies focus on health? How do companies try to promote unhealthy products?

GRAMMAR

Determiners and quantifiers

A **Work in pairs. Read the sentences. Which of the determiners or quantifiers in bold describe 100%, a large amount, a medium to small amount or 0%?**

1. There's **little** evidence to support many of the health claims made about yogurt.
2. You need **plenty of** fruits and vegetables in your diet.
3. It's not true that we need to drink **several** glasses of water a day.
4. There is **no** evidence to support that claim.
5. **All** companies have to be careful with the wording of their ads.
6. **Neither** ad was particularly accurate.
7. **Every** claim must be supported by evidence.
8. There isn't really **any** evidence to support that claim.
9. **None** of those claims are based on real data.

B **WORK IT OUT** **Choose the correct options to complete the rules.**

Determiners and quantifiers

few, much, many, a little, etc

- We use *many, few, a few, several, a large number of* with [1]***countable / uncountable / countable and uncountable*** nouns.
- We use *much, a little, little, a great deal of, a large amount of* with [2]***countable / uncountable / countable and uncountable*** nouns.
- We use *a lot of, lots of, plenty of, some* and *any* with [3]***countable / uncountable / countable and uncountable*** nouns.

all, each and ***every***

- We use *all* with [4]***singular / plural*** nouns.
- We use *each* and *every* with [5]***singular / plural*** nouns.

both, either and ***neither***

- We use *both* with [6]***singular / plural*** nouns.
- We use *either* and *neither* with [7]***singular / plural*** nouns.

no, none and ***any***

- We use *no* + noun in [8]***positive / negative*** sentences and *any* + noun in [9]***positive / negative*** sentences.
- We use *none* in short answers, in [10]***positive / negative*** sentences, or with *of* + pronoun / countable or uncountable nouns.

C Go to the **Grammar Hub** on **page XII**.

PRONUNCIATION

Connected speech: determiners and quantifiers

9.6 **A** **Listen to the extracts from the radio show. Is there a pause between the words in bold? Is the pronunciation of *of* strong or weak?**

1. We get **plenty of water** through food.
2. You'd have to eat **a lot of** fruit to get the same amount of sugar as you'd get from, say, a soda.

9.7 **B** **Draw (‿) to show the connected speech in the determiners and quantifiers below. Then listen and check.**

1. A large number of people pay attention to claims in advertising.
2. A lot of people are influenced by product reviews.
3. Plenty of respondents don't pay attention to the wording of an ad.
4. A few of the people interviewed said that price wasn't a factor when choosing clothes.
5. Hundreds of people buy products because of celebrity endorsements.

SPEAKING

A **PLAN** **Work in pairs. You are going to conduct a survey on factors that influence people's shopping habits. Adapt the sample questions to fit one of the topics in the box.**

clothes food vacations technology

1 **Do you regularly eat out in restaurants? Yes/No**

2 **Which factors are the most important when choosing a restaurant?**

	not significant						significant
price	1	2	3	4	5	6	7
location	1	2	3	4	5	6	7
décor	1	2	3	4	5	6	7
type of food	1	2	3	4	5	6	7

3 **Restaurant reviews have an influence on my choice of restaurant.**

strongly agree — agree — neutral — disagree — strongly disagree

4 **Which ONE of these has the most influence when you write your own review of a restaurant?**

value for money service quality of the food

B **SPEAK** **Ask your questions from Exercise A to as many people as possible in ten minutes. Write down their answers.**

C **DISCUSS** **Work in pairs. Analyze your answers from Exercise B.**

Our results show that the most important thing when eating out is the quality of the food …

D **PRESENT** **Present your findings to the class.**

OPRAH WINFREY

- founder of The Oprah Winfrey Network (OWN)
- grew up in extreme poverty
- net worth = $2.9 billion

JEFF BEZOS

- co-founder of Amazon
- quit a well-paid job on Wall Street to develop Amazon
- net worth = $157.4 billion

ZHOU QUNFEI

- founder of Lens Technology
- left school at 16 to work in a factory
- net worth = $5.4 billion

READING

A SPEAK Work in groups. Look at the infographic and discuss the questions.

1 Can you think of any other famous entrepreneurs? What products or services did they create?

2 What qualities do you think make a good entrepreneur?

3 Would you like to start your own business? Why/Why not?

B READ FOR GIST Read *The path to success* and choose the best sub-heading (1–3).

1 Setting up a new fashion label can be difficult, especially with minimal advertising.

2 How the courage to follow a childhood dream led to an international success story.

3 How celebrities can help promote your values.

C TOPIC SENTENCES Read the article again. Match the topic sentences (1–5) to the blanks (a–e). Use the information in the box to help you.

> **Topic sentences**
>
> Topic sentences express the main idea of a paragraph. They are usually found at the beginning of a paragraph and are frequently supported by further related information or examples. Identifying topic sentences can help you get a quick overall understanding of a text without having to read in detail.

1 The brand has since become known for its colorful floral prints, which are inspired by Nicola's happy childhood memories of the summer in the English countryside.

2 The story of many successful entrepreneurs is the stuff of Hollywood – rags-to-riches tales of people who overcame great challenges in order to succeed.

3 In an age where so many of us seem content to remain in well-paid, but ultimately dissatisfying jobs, it's refreshing to see someone have the courage to make a dramatic lifestyle change.

4 Yet like many of us, Nicola felt that something was missing and decided to do something about it.

5 In the past decade, Beautiful Soul has used a variety of techniques to raise brand awareness.

THE PATH TO SUCCESS

a ___ Oprah Winfrey was born into extreme poverty, yet recently became the world's first black female billionaire. Bill Gates and Mark Zuckerburg both dropped out of college, but went on to create two of the most influential companies in modern history. Starting out on the wrong foot seems to be the inspiration many entrepreneurs need to create an empire, and Nicola Woods is no exception. For 11 years, Nicola built a successful career in the fast-paced world of corporate insurance. She wore designer clothing, drove sports cars and went on dream vacations.

b ___ Looking for inspiration, she took a six-month sabbatical to travel around the world. Sitting among the cherry blossom in a park in central Tokyo, Nicola's thoughts turned to her childhood dream of working in the fashion industry. Realizing that she needed a radical change of lifestyle, Nicola enrolled in college and earned a BA in Fashion, Design and Technology. She then went on to launch the luxury womenswear **brand**, Beautiful Soul, in 2008.

D READ FOR DETAIL Read the article again and answer the questions. Underline the parts of the text that give you the answers.

1 Why did Nicola take six months off work to go traveling?
2 What lifestyle change did Nicola make when she returned from Japan?
3 Which two values is the brand built upon?
4 How do these values influence their use of materials?
5 Who has helped to raise the brand's international profile?
6 What has brought the company to the attention of the media?
7 What do the private fittings allow Nicola to do?
8 What does the writer think Nicola should be congratulated for?

E SPEAK Work in groups. Nicola had a successful career in corporate insurance that made her wealthy, yet she was still dissatisfied. What do you think are the most important factors in career satisfaction?

c ___ Her clothes are proudly feminine and offer a modern interpretation of classic British designs. However, maybe as interesting as the designs themselves are the values that lie behind them. There is an industry-wide **trend** toward clothing that does not damage the environment and Nicola is excited to lead the charge. The brand is committed to sustainability and the regeneration of the British manufacturing and textiles industries. Materials are organic, locally sourced and fair trade, proving to the **consumer** that luxury clothing can still be produced ethically. The company also operates a zero-waste policy, using leftover fabric from one season in the creation of the next.

d ___ Rather than expensive **ad campaigns**, the fashion label has largely relied on word of mouth, driven to a large extent by the support of **high-profile** celebrities. Pippa Middleton, Taylor Swift and Katy Perry are among those to publicly **endorse** the brand, helping to raise its international profile. Beautiful Soul has also attracted vast media attention through its involvement in the London, Milan and Paris fashion weeks and is now stocked at high-end boutiques around the world. However, Nicola is also eager to connect with her customers face-to-face, so the brand has recently begun offering private fittings at their studio in Portobello, West London. The hope is that **marketing strategies** like these, as well as studio open days, will allow Nicola to better understand her **target market** and adapt accordingly.

e ___ Nicola Woods may not have been born into poverty, nor did she drop out of college before becoming successful. Yet like all entrepreneurs, she too had to show great strength of character to get where she is today.

Glossary

fair trade (n) a system that ensures the original producer receives a fair price for their goods
sabbatical (n) a period of time when someone (usually a college professor) is allowed to stop working in order to travel or study
sustainability (n) the use of methods that cause little to no damage to the environment and can therefore continue for a long period of time

VOCABULARY
Advertising

A Scan the article again. Complete the definitions with the words in bold.

1 ________________ (n) a series of advertisements that share a single idea or theme
2 ________________ (n) a plan of how to encourage people to buy a product or service
3 ________________ (n) someone who buys or uses goods and services
4 ________________ (v) to express support for someone or something, especially in public
5 ________________ (n) a product or group of products that has its own name and is made by one company
6 ________________ (n) the group of people that a product or service is directed toward
7 ________________ (adj) frequently seen in public, mentioned in newspapers or appearing on television
8 ________________ (n) a gradual development or change in a situation

B Complete the sentences with the correct form of the words in Exercise A.

1 Which recent TV ________________ do you think have been most effective? Why?
2 Do you think ________________ celebrities should be involved in advertising? Why/Why not?
3 Are you more likely to buy a product if it's ________________ by a celebrity? Why/Why not?
4 Who do you think is the ________________ for the following products – energy drinks, electric cars, video game consoles, high-end sports equipment? Why?
5 Which ________________ do you associate with luxury and quality? Why?
6 How can ________________ influence the way products or services are advertised?
7 Which ________________ would discourage you from buying a product or service? Why?
8 Do you follow the latest fashion ________________? Why/Why not?

C SPEAK Work in pairs. Ask and answer the questions in Exercise B.

SPEAKING HUB

A PLAN Work in groups. Go to the Communication Hub on page XXI.

B PRESENT Present your campaign to the class and answer their follow-up questions.

Conduct a survey about what influences our purchases

Design and present an ad campaign

Café Hub

9.3 Raising capital

A – illustrating your argument S – reformulating and paraphrasing

Crowdfunding

Glossary

film (n) (British) = movie (n) (American)

COMPREHENSION

A **Work in pairs. What do you think is the best way to raise money for a new business or project? Why?**

Glossary

commission (n) a payment made to someone that is directly related to the amount they sell of something

donor (n) someone who gives money or goods to an organization that needs help

B **Watch a news report about getting investment for new projects. Answer the questions.**

1 How did the director raise money for his film?

2 How does this system work?

3 Why do people donate money like this?

C 00:00–01:42 **Watch the first part of the report again. Are these sentences true (T) or false (F)? Correct the false sentences.**

1 The director produced a video about the project as part of his Kickstarter campaign. *T / F*

2 To date, the campaign has raised over two thousand dollars more than its original goal. *T / F*

3 Some donors are given the opportunity to appear in the films they support. *T / F*

4 Kickstarter only makes money if a project is successful. *T / F*

D 01:43–02:37 **Watch the second part of the report again. Choose the best options to complete the sentences.**

1 Kickstarter CEO, Yancey Strickler, says most ideas ***wouldn't be profitable / aren't interesting*** enough to gain traditional investment.

2 Michael Moore has ***successfully funded projects on / publicly endorsed*** Kickstarter.

3 Moore states that he ***would be happy to invest / has previously invested*** in film projects via Kickstarter.

4 A major issue of crowdfunding is that many projects ***are never finished / cost more than estimated***.

AUTHENTIC ENGLISH

A **Work in pairs. Read the extract from the report. What is the speaker's main argument? How does he illustrate it?**

99% of ideas will never be a good fit for investment because they're not going to make a lot of money. But if instead the notion is, 'What do we want to see exist? What do we think would be cool and interesting? What would we want to see?', there's a lot more things that become possible.

B **Match the arguments (1–3) with the questions that could be used to illustrate them (a–c). Use the information in the box to help you.**

Illustrating your argument

In natural spoken English, we frequently ask rhetorical questions to emphasize or support our arguments:

We have to ask ourselves, 'What do we want to highlight about our project? How can people benefit from supporting us?'

1 Almost two thirds of the people surveyed still believe Vitamin C cures the common cold.

2 The results of the survey indicate that unemployment is still on the rise.

3 Over the past year, we've seen a 60% increase in profits.

a The obvious question is, 'What influenced such a positive performance?'

b Which begs the question, 'What steps can be taken to get people back into work?'

c This raises the question, 'How can we better inform the public?'

C **Work in pairs. Take turns making sentences about the topics below, then illustrating your ideas with a question.**

- sports
- health
- employment

A: Arsenal has admitted that they need a better striker to compete at the highest level.

B: The only question is, 'How much are they willing to pay for one?'

Starting positions

A Work in pairs. Think of the steps that are involved in starting a new business. What order do they have to be done in?

B Watch the video. Choose the best summary (1 or 2).

1 Inspired by Sam's advice, Emily decides to take a traditional route to funding her new business venture.

2 Despite Sam's advice, Emily decides to take a more modern approach to funding her new business venture.

SPEAKING SKILL

A Watch the video again. Answer the questions.

1 What is the function of the phrases *I just meant …*, *What I meant to say was …* and *What I meant is …*?

2 What is the function of *essentially* and *basically*?

B Read the information in the box and check your answers to Exercise A.

Reformulating and paraphrasing

Sometimes in conversation we need to explain something in a different way to help the listener understand. This is called reformulating.

To do this, we use phrases such as: *I just mean (that) …*, *What I'm trying to say is …*, *What I meant to say was …*, *In other words …*, *What I mean is (that) …*, *That's to say …*

Sometimes the listener doesn't understand because we've used a word or phrase that they're unfamiliar with. Rather than give a long explanation, we usually focus on the essential details. This is called paraphrasing.

To do this, we use phrases such as: *(So) essentially/basically …*

C Choose a topic that you know a lot about (e.g. a particular subject, sport, etc) and brainstorm a list of interesting, technical terms associated with it.

D Work in pairs. Tell each other about the topic you chose in Exercise A, using technical language. Reformulate or paraphrase when necessary.

SPEAKING HUB

A PREPARE Look at the following ideas that people are hoping to crowdfund. Brainstorm the strengths and weaknesses of each.

- Idea A: a chip that is inserted in your brain to allow you to access the internet with your mind. Will allow users to access the internet instantly without using a device. Will be very expensive.
- Idea B: wireless electricity. No more power cables in the home or across the country. There are concerns about electromagnetic radiation damaging people's health.
- Idea C: a tablet that turns a container of ocean water into drinking water. Will help stop water shortages. Production process of tablets creates toxic pollution.

B SPEAK Work in groups. You have $50,000 to invest in crowdfunding projects. Discuss each of the projects in Exercise A and decide how much, if anything, to invest in them.

We should be asking, 'Which idea is tackling the most important issue of the day?' And it seems to me that renewable energy is the most important.

C REFLECT As a class, discuss which ideas got the most/least funding and why.

Discuss investment opportunities

➤ Turn to page XXVI to learn how to write a proposal.

Unit 9 Review

VOCABULARY

A Match the numbers (1–8) to the letters (a–h) to form full sentences.

1 I am responsible …
2 Our brand is associated …
3 All of our products are made …
4 I'm sick …
5 It is important for businesses to show that they care …
6 When the dress arrived, I was really dissatisfied …
7 The success of a company is dependent …
8 I'm interested …

a with luxury and success.
b with it. It looked nothing like the pictures.
c from locally sourced materials.
d on many factors.
e for a team of 20 people at work.
f about the people who work for them.
g in the idea of moving to a new house but my husband wants to stay where we are.
h of people on social media showing off about their lives.

B Complete the text with the words in the box.

analysis data evidence researchers theory

The pursuit of happiness

For decades, the simplest way to address unhappiness has been to go shopping. But does retail therapy actually work? Can we buy our way to happiness?

To test the [1] ______________, a group of [2] ______________ from the Institute for Social Sciences interviewed thousands of shoppers before and after a spending spree. [3] ______________ of the [4] ______________ seemed to indicate that retail therapy does make us happier immediately after the purchase. However, as yet, there is no [5] ______________ to suggest that shopping can buy you long-term happiness. The key to this, it seems, remains a mystery!

C Work in groups. Discuss the questions.

1 Why do you think people frequently continue to believe something, despite a large amount of scientific evidence against it?
2 What kind of research do you think governments should fund? Why?

D Choose the correct options (a, b or c) to complete the sentences.

1 To work in fashion, it's important to keep up with ___ and influencers.
a brands b trends c campaigns
2 We are trying to ___ young males from a professional background.
a target b advertise c campaign
3 ___ social media stars are paid a lot of money to advertise particular brands.
a Consumers b High-profile c Trend
4 We hired six athletes to ___ our new health-food range.
a campaign b target c endorse
5 Our company is going to try to raise our ___ awareness by sponsoring national sporting events.
a campaign b advertise c brand
6 ___ frequently buy products that represent a certain lifestyle.
a Consumers b Brands c High profile

E Work in pairs. Discuss the questions.

1 Which brands are you most loyal to? Why?
2 How can consumers influence the products and services they use?
3 Which products do you think are marketed at your age range? Why?

GRAMMAR

A Rewrite the sentences as one sentence using an adjective clause. Leave out the relative pronoun where possible.

1 Have you read the book? The one I lent you.
Have ______________________________?
2 There was some leftover pizza in the fridge. Where is it?
Where's ______________________________?
3 That's the boy. His brother has joined our soccer team.
That's ______________________________.
4 I bought a new cell phone. It's really good.
The ______________________________.
5 Here's the beach. My family had our first vacation here.
This is ______________________________.

B Are these sentences correct or incorrect? Rewrite the incorrect sentences.

1 I think every city should have bike lanes.
2 It was a great game of tennis. Either players played amazingly.
3 Any of you can leave until the exam is finished.
4 Every person is influenced by advertising to at least some degree.
5 Not many people came. Just few friends from college.
6 We haven't received any positive reviews for over a week.
7 I'm happy with neither restaurant since both look nice.
8 Did you do many sightseeing on vacation?

10 MEDIA

Ignorance, the root and stem of all evil.

Plato

A Japanese commuter on the Yamanote Rail Line in Tokyo, Japan.

OBJECTIVES

- give opinions on recent news stories
- intervene appropriately in a discussion
- report a conversation
- plan and create a viral marketing ad
- give your opinion on streaming services
- write a persuasive essay

Work with a partner. Discuss the questions.

1. Read the quote. Do you think the internet makes us more or less ignorant? Why?
2. Should the media respect the privacy of famous people? Why/Why not?
3. What media sources do you read on a regular basis? Why do you read those ones?

10.1 Reporting the news

- Give opinions on recent news stories
- Intervene appropriately in a discussion

G – reported speech S – listening for repair and elaboration V – traditional media P – avoiding interruption

READING

A SPEAK Work in pairs. Discuss the questions below.

1 When was the last time you bought a magazine or newspaper?

2 Why do you think people now get more of their news online than in the traditional media?

10.1 **B Listen to a press conference with the editor of a lifestyle magazine called *Healthy Me*. Answer the questions.**

1 What is the announcement about?
 a a new print and digital magazine coming out
 b a print magazine becoming digital-only
 c an online magazine releasing a print version

2 What trend inspired the new business model?
 a the increased popularity of digital content in general
 b the increased popularity of the magazine
 c the increased popularity of health-based apps

3 According to the speaker, what type of print media will be affected by digital?
 a lifestyle magazines
 b fiction
 c reference books

C READ FOR MAIN IDEA Read *The death of print?* and choose the best summary of the writer's opinion (1–3).

1 The shift toward digital content is the beginning of the end for print products.

2 Sales of print products may actually be improved by the shift toward digital content.

3 Despite the shift toward digital content, there is still a market for print products.

D READ FOR DETAIL Read the article again and answer the questions. Underline the parts of the text that give you the answers.

1 What two things prompted LMI Media to make their magazine digital-only?

2 What method do online publications use to try to generate income?

3 How do the public feel about this?

4 What type of magazine is thriving?

5 What type of magazine does the author think will struggle?

6 What types of print media are still successful?

E SPEAK Work in groups. Discuss the questions.

1 Do you prefer print or digital media? Why?

2 What type of magazines, if any, do you think will survive in the future?

3 Do you think all online content should be free? Why/Why not?

GRAMMAR

Reported speech

A Scan the article again. Underline the reported speech that matches the following extracts from the press conference.

1 'We've gone from a distribution of just over 500,000 copies a month to under 100,000.'

2 'In fact, yesterday saw the total number of registered users reach over one million.'

3 'Will other publications from LMI Media make the same transition?'

4 'I'm sure all magazine publishers will start to re-evaluate their options over the next five to ten years.'

5 'What does this trend mean for print media in general?'

6 'However, for lifestyle magazines like ours, which are predominantly directed toward a younger audience, it simply doesn't make any financial sense to produce print media any longer.'

The DEATH of PRINT?

Lucy Morgan | 04/29/2019

As *Healthy Me* becomes the latest high-profile magazine to abandon print, Lucy Morgan makes the case against the digital revolution.

LMI Media has recently announced that January's issue of the lifestyle magazine *Healthy Me* will be the final print edition, making it the latest in a long line of publications to go digital-only. Yet is this really the right approach or do print magazines simply need to adapt to the changing marketplace?

B WORK IT OUT Complete the rules in the box. Use the examples in Exercise A to help you.

Reported speech

- When we report what someone said, we usually change the verb by moving it back one tense into the past.
  - present progressive → past progressive
  - simple past / present perfect → [1] ________________
  - *will* → [2] ________________
  - *can* → *could*
- We usually need to change time and place references.
  - *yesterday* → [3] ________________
  - *here* → *there*
- It isn't necessary to change the tense when:
  - the information is still true or relevant now.
  - the reporting verb is in the [4] ________________ tense.
- When we report questions, we don't use the auxiliary verb [5] ________________.
- With *yes/no* questions we use *if* or [6] ________________.

C Go to the **Grammar Hub** on **page XIV**.

D SPEAK Work in pairs. Use the prompts below to interview your partner about their print and digital reading habits. Write notes about their answers.

- How often / read magazines?
- Which magazines?
- Print or digital? Why?
- Which / online magazines?

E DISCUSS Work in groups. Report your findings from Exercise D. What similarities or trends can you identify?

SPEAKING

A PLAN Think about an interesting news story you read recently. Write notes about:

- the main ideas / key events
- things that people said

B SPEAK Work in pairs. Explain your news stories and give your opinions on them.

In a press conference yesterday morning, an emotional Sally Ronson, editor-in-chief of *Healthy Me*, stated that a combination of declining sales over the past five years and the increased popularity of digital content had motivated the change. She told reporters that the publication had gone from a distribution of just over 500,000 copies a month to under 100,000 – a huge number of readers to lose in such a short period of time. However, the magazine is still popular. Since 2014, downloads of the *Healthy Me* app have increased by 300%. In fact, Ronson said that the previous day had seen the total number of registered users reach over one million. The issue for publications like this is how to turn this interest into sales. One method is to introduce paywalls – a feature in an app or website that stops people who have not paid a subscription from accessing some or all of the content. However, the general perception of the public seems to be that online content should be free and, as a result, few are willing to pay to access their favorite publications.

When asked whether other publications from LMI Media would make the same transition, Ronson said no. Yet it's clear that she believes the future of magazine publishing is digital. In fact, she said she was sure that all magazine publishers would start to re-evaluate their options over the next five to ten years. However, I'm not sure this is true. Magazines with highly specialized content, such as the *Spectator*, *The Economist* and *Prospect* have all seen significant growth. However, I do agree with Ronson when she says that for lifestyle magazines like hers, which are predominantly directed toward a younger audience, it simply doesn't make any financial sense to produce print media any longer. Not surprisingly, people aren't willing to pay for 'empty' news about barely famous people or to read articles about serious content produced by barely credible journalists.

The press also asked Ronson what this digital trend meant for print media in general and she very rightly pointed out that this depends entirely on the type of publication. Print media is thriving in many areas. E-book sales are now falling while the sales of printed fiction are actually increasing. E-books also never really had any serious impact on the sales of reference books. Furthermore, local papers with content focused on a small region still tend to be popular.

Magazines and newspapers will no doubt have to evolve and those that do so innovatively will prosper. Those that focus on celebrity gossip and news found more easily on the internet will almost certainly disappear, but specialist magazines and local news are likely to continue to thrive.

LISTENING

A SPEAK Work in pairs. Look at the news headlines and discuss which you think are from real news stories and which are fake.

B PREDICT Work in groups. How big is the problem of fake news? What can be done to help people deal with fake news?

10.2 **C LISTEN FOR GIST** Listen to an interview with a journalist about fake news. Do they mention any of your ideas from Exercise B?

10.2 **D LISTEN FOR DETAIL** Listen again. Complete the sentences with no more than three words from the interview.

1 Some fake news is for fun but many articles want you to believe the content is ________________ news.
2 The internet, specifically ________________, has changed the way we consume media.
3 Internet advertising comes from ________________ understanding the things you read and look at.
4 People have less ________________ in sources like CNN or the BBC than they used to.
5 People rarely ________________ behind the stories they read.
6 Teaching students ________________ would help them better identify fake news.

10.2 **E LISTEN FOR REPAIR AND ELABORATION** Listen again. Are these sentences true (T) or false (F)? Correct the false sentences. Use the information in the box to help you.

> **Listening for repair and elaboration**
>
> In presentations and interviews, speakers sometimes make mistakes and need to correct themselves. When making a repair like this, we frequently use phrases such as:
>
> *Let me rephrase that …, Sorry, what I meant to say was …*
>
> At other points, the speaker may feel that their point has been misunderstood and try to give more detail or explain something in a different way. When elaborating like this, we frequently use phrases such as:
>
> *What I mean is …, In other words …, To be more precise …*

According to the speaker …

1 it's easier to publish fake news online. *T / F*
2 opinion has no place in real journalism. *T / F*
3 there is no agreement on the extent of the damage climate change will cause. *T / F*
4 the government is ultimately responsible for content published online. *T / F*
5 75% of students can't spot fake news. *T / F*

F SPEAK Work in groups. Discuss the questions.

1 Have you ever been tricked by fake news?
2 Whose responsibility is it to deal with fake news?
3 Do you think it should be illegal to publish fake news stories? Why/Why not?

VOCABULARY
Traditional media

A Complete the definitions with the words in bold.

1 The **editor** lost his job after the paper was accused of publishing fake news.
2 The **headline** was misleading because it said they had found a long-term cure.
3 **Tabloid** newspapers are mainly full of photos and celebrity gossip.
4 The press **coverage** of the royal wedding lasted all day.
5 The newspaper was accused of being **biased** in favor of the president.
6 The journalist refused to reveal the **source** of their story.
7 Her views are highly **subjective** and rarely based on hard evidence.
8 The **broadsheet** newspapers all included an in-depth analysis of the situation.

a ________________ (n) a small newspaper with a lot of pictures and short articles, frequently about famous people
b ________________ (n) the way news is reported on television or radio or in the newspapers
c ________________ (n) a person who is in charge of a newspaper or magazine
d ________________ (n) where information comes from
e ________________ (adj) based on your own feelings and beliefs, not facts
f ________________ (n) a large newspaper generally considered to be more serious than smaller newspapers
g ________________ (adj) preferring one person, thing, or idea to another in a way that is unfair
h ________________ (n) the title of a newspaper story that is printed in large letters

B Complete the questions with the correct form of the words in Exercise A.

1 Is it OK for journalists to write articles that are ________________ or should they be objective?
2 Do you prefer to read serious ________________ newspapers or less serious ________________ papers?
3 Should an ________________ take responsibility for all stories in their paper?
4 Sensationalist ________________ are written to encourage people to buy papers and click on articles online. Should they be banned?
5 Should press ________________ of people's lives be controlled to allow more privacy?
6 Why should we pay attention to the ________________ of a newspaper article?
7 Newspapers are frequently ________________ toward certain political parties. Should this be banned?

C SPEAK Work in pairs. Discuss the questions in Exercise B. Explain your reasoning.

PRONUNCIATION
Avoiding interruption

10.3 **A Listen to this extract from the interview. What intonation is used on the highlighted words – falling (↘) or rise-fall-rise (↗↘↗)? Why?**

I think we used to have more faith in sources like CNN, but now people don't know who to trust.

10.4 **B Underline the word(s) you think will have a rise-fall-rise tone. Then listen and check.**

1 Governments need to take much stronger action against companies that circulate fake news stories; it's just not OK to misinform the public.
2 In other words, unlike bloggers and people writing on social media, large newspapers can't just lie or make things up.

SPEAKING HUB

A PLAN Read the questions. Write notes about your opinions on the following questions:

1 Do large media organizations have too much influence?
2 Do you think the government should be involved in making sure the media isn't biased?
3 What are the advantages and disadvantages of people getting news from the internet?
4 Whose responsibility is it to fact-check content that is produced online?
5 Do you think less fake news would exist if the individual writers were held responsible for the content they produced?
6 Do you think journalists and the media should be allowed to say they can't reveal their sources?

B PREPARE Think about other possible viewpoints and how you would respond to them.

C SPEAK Work in groups. Take turns answering the questions while politely waiting for an opportunity to ask a follow-up question to explore different points of view.

- Give opinions on recent news stories
- Intervene appropriately in a discussion

10.2 Digital media

- Report a conversation
- Plan and create a viral marketing ad

S – substitution
V – social media; adjective + noun collocations
G – reporting verbs
P – using intonation to attract and keep interest

READING

A SPEAK Work in groups. Discuss the questions.

1 How do you know that an article you are reading comes from a credible source?

2 How can your own bias affect what you read and how you interpret it?

B PREDICT Work in pairs. Read the headlines from three different news stories and look at the pictures. What do you think each story is about?

C SKIM Skim the news stories and check your predictions from Exercise B.

D SUBSTITUTION Read again. What do the words in bold refer to? Use the information in the box to help you.

Substitution

To avoid repetition, writers frequently replace phrases, clauses or ideas with other words. This is called substitution. Common substitutes are:

- *one, ones, some*
  *There are many reasons to doubt the statement, but **one** of the most important is that the timings just don't add up.*
  (*one* = a reason to doubt the statement)
- *do*
  *While Mr. Evans didn't have access to the property, the investigation has revealed that his partner **did**.*
  (*did* = have access to the property)
- *either/neither*
  *I've never seen him before in my life. **Neither** has my husband.*
  (*neither* = not seen him before)

1 '... but apparently Mr. Rodriguez **did**.'

2 '**Some** even work all night...'

3 '... yet **neither** have been named as part of the investigation.'

4 '... **one** being how the chocolate could have possibly survived for over 3,000 years.'

5 'Believe me, **so do I**.'

E SPEAK Work in groups. Do you think any of the stories are true? Why/Why not?

GRAMMAR

Reporting verbs

A Read the news stories again. Match the highlighted sentences (1–5) to the direct speech (a–e).

a 'No, I'm sorry. I cannot discuss an on-going investigation.' ___

b 'We simply need to run a lot of tests. Until then, this is nothing more than a fun news item.' ___

c 'I'm sorry the police were called out unnecessarily.' ___

d 'That's correct. The animal was delivered home safely.' ___

e 'Earlier today my team discovered two additional bars nearby – both in a similar state.' ___

Terrified New Yorker sees 'bear'
CALLS 911

Brooklyn Heights, New York –

Brooklyn Heights resident Anthony Rodriguez was terrified to see a bear rummaging through the trash cans outside his apartment early yesterday morning. Rodriguez called the NYPD and officers were soon at the scene. Fortunately for attending officers Liam Henderson and Alyssa Romano, the 'bear' turned out to be a hungry but harmless domestic dog. 'We arrived at approximately 6:30 am to find a large brown dog checking trash cans on the street for leftover food,' Officer Romano told reporters. She added, 'I have no idea how anyone could confuse the animal for a bear, but apparently Mr. Rodriguez did. [1]Rodriguez later apologized for wasting police time. The story has prompted a number of animal rights groups to raise concerns over the dog's welfare. [2]In response, a spokesperson for the police department confirmed that the animal had been safely returned to its owners.

TECH CRIMINAL CAUGHT HANGING AROUND

An employee of IT giant FTP Systems was arrested last night following a failed burglary attempt at the company's head office.

Neil Aitken broke into the London office shortly after midnight in order to steal sensitive computer data. Having downloaded over five terabytes of confidential information to his personal laptop, Mr. Aitken got stuck in the elevator on the 54th floor and was forced to use the alarm to call for help. 'I wasn't surprised to hear the alarm,' said Geoff Payton, the maintenance worker on duty that night. 'A lot of programmers work late and some even work all night. But Mr. Aitken kept asking me not to call the police, which seemed suspicious, so I called the authorities.' When Mr. Aitken was finally rescued from the elevator over two hours later, he was promptly arrested and will stand trial for burglary next month. [3]Although investigators have refused to comment on their current progress, it is widely believed that Mr. Aitken had intended to sell the stolen data to FTP Systems' biggest competitor, BIOS Technologies. Our sources have also suggested that the police are eager to talk to two current employees of BIOS Technologies, about their dealings with Mr. Aitken, yet neither has been named as part of the investigation.

EGYPTIAN DISCOVERY MAY CHANGE THE HISTORY OF CHOCOLATE

Human civilization has a long history with chocolate. As far back as 1900 BCE, the Mayans of Central America prepared a bitter, frothy drink with crushed cocoa beans, cornmeal and chili peppers. The Aztecs used cocoa beans as currency and drank chocolate at royal feasts.

However, it wasn't until 1847 that Fry & Sons produced the first bar of chocolate as we know it. At least, that's what historians thought until a ground-breaking discovery made 10 km north of Cairo last month.

A team of archeologists digging outside the tomb of a wealthy Egyptian official from the 13th century were amazed to find what appeared to be several ancient chocolate bars buried in the sand. 'We discovered four bars in total, each wrapped in white fabric,' explained lead researcher Arnaud Laurent. 'Each bar appears to be divided into five sections, maybe to make them easier to eat.' [4]Laurent later informed local journalists that his team had found two more bars in a similar condition.

Although images of all six chocolate bars have been widely shared online, not everyone is convinced of their authenticity. In an article published in the Journal of Archaeological Studies, [5]Professor Richard Hamilton advised historians not to take the discovery seriously until further research has been conducted. 'It's certainly an interesting discovery,' writes Professor Hamilton, 'but there are still a lot of things we don't know – one being how the chocolate could have possibly survived for over 3,000 years.' In a response on Twitter posted late last night, Laurent wrote, 'Everyone has a lot of questions. Believe me, so do I.'

B WORK IT OUT Complete the rules with verbs from Exercise A.

Reporting verbs

We can use reporting verbs to explain the way in which something was said. Reporting verbs are followed by a range of different structures:

a *argue,* [1] ____________, *state, suggest* + (*that*) + clause

b *assure,* [2] ____________, *tell, warn* + object + (*that*)

c *agree, demand, offer,* [3] ____________, *threaten* + infinitive

d [4] ____________, *encourage, persuade, remind, warn, convince* + object + infinitive

e *admit,* [5] ____________, *deny, insist, suggest* + (preposition) + verb + *-ing*

C Go to the **Grammar Hub** on **page XIV**.

D PRACTICE Rewrite the quotes in reported speech using the verbs in the box.

apologize blame encourage refuse threaten

1 'We won't leave until our demands are met.'
The protestors ____________________.

2 'We will fire any employee who is one minute late.'
The company ____________________.

3 'We want to say we're sorry to the 100 people who got food poisoning last week.'
The restaurant ____________________.

4 'Can anyone who saw anything please contact us?'
The police ____________________.

5 'The service is slow because of the internet provider.'
The TV company ____________________.

SPEAKING

A PLAN You are going to discuss the following questions with a partner. You must tell the truth in response to three of the questions and lie in response to the other. Write notes about what you want to say.

1 Have you ever blamed someone else for something that you did?

2 Have you ever cheated on a test?

3 What's your biggest regret?

4 Have you ever been persuaded to do something stupid?

B SPEAK Work in pairs. Discuss the questions in Exercise A. Remember to tell one lie.

C DISCUSS Work with another pair. Report your partner's answers from Exercise B and explain which one you think was a lie and why.

Luis denied ever cheating on a test, but that can't be true!

VOCABULARY
Social media

A Work in pairs. Look at the pictures (1–3). What do they have in common? Have you done any of these things?

B Complete the definitions with the correct form of the words in bold in *#nomakeupselfie*.

1 When something goes ________________ it becomes very popular and spreads quickly, especially on the internet.

2 A ________________ is a series of organized activities designed to achieve a particular social, commercial or political result.

3 When something is ________________, it is frequently being mentioned or discussed on the internet, particularly on social media platforms.

4 To ________________ people with a message or program means they see or hear it.

5 A ________________ is someone who chooses to receive updates and messages from another person on a social media platform.

6 A ________________ is a symbol used on social media to describe the general subject of a post.

7 An ________________ is someone who changes the way people behave, especially through social media.

#nomakeupselfie

The no make-up selfie **campaign** was developed to raise awareness of cancer research in the UK. The **hashtag** nomakeupselfie started **trending** on various social media websites asking women to post a selfie with no make-up and to donate money to Cancer Research UK. The campaign quickly spread across the internet especially when celebrities such as Lady Gaga, Alicia Keys and Heidi Klum also shared selfies with their **followers** on Instagram. This, along with other social media **influencers** following suit, helped the campaign to **reach** a much wider audience. The trend went **viral** and donations reached $8 million in six days.

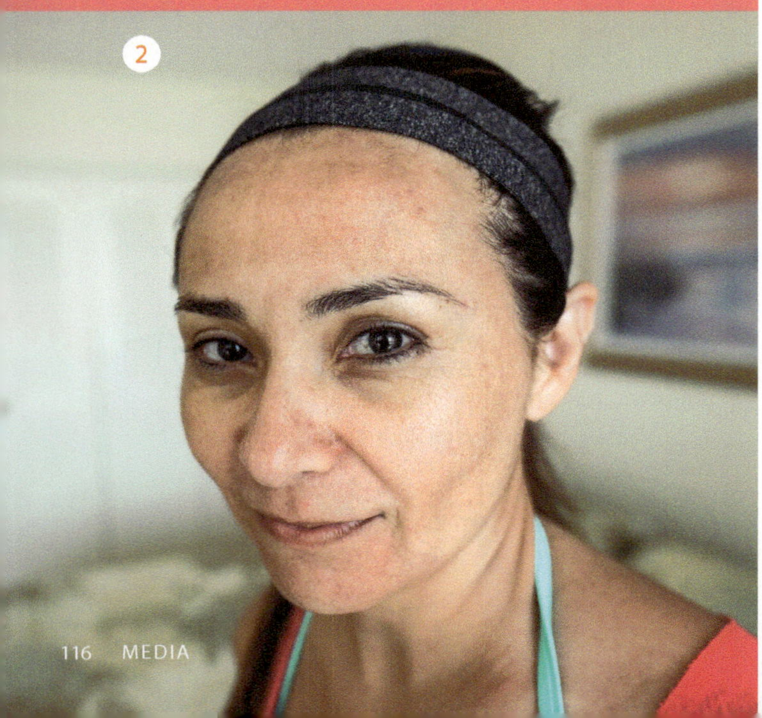

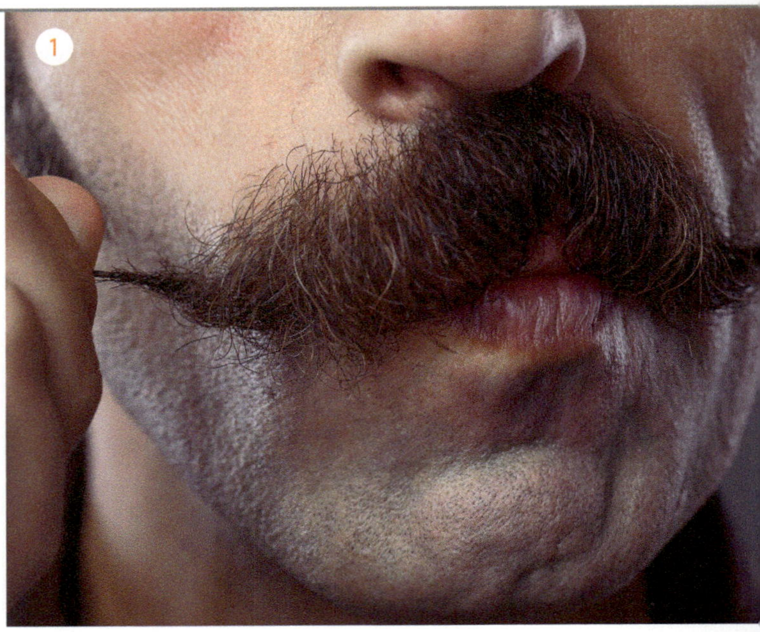

C Go to the **Vocabulary Hub** on page **XVII**.

D SPEAK Work in groups. Discuss the questions.

1 Who do you follow on social media? Why?

2 Which hashtags have you seen trending lately?

3 What do you think makes a campaign go viral?

LISTENING

10.5 **A LISTEN FOR ORGANIZATION** Listen to a talk on viral marketing campaigns. Put the topics in the order they're discussed.

___ the research behind viral success
___ create content which affects people's emotions
___ successful charity campaigns that went viral
___ understand the people you are hoping to reach
___ social media influencers can help raise awareness
___ build relationships with donors to ensure long-term success

10.5 **B LISTEN FOR DETAIL** Listen again. Complete the sentences with no more than three words or a number from the talk.

1 The Ice Bucket Challenge had ________________ mentions online and 15 million videos were watched ________________ times online.

2 People will react similarly when they see an ________________.

3 The speaker suggests using Pinterest in a campaign directed toward younger ________________.

4 Videos go viral when they affect people's ________________.

5 Frequent ________________ are integral to a charity's continued success.

6 A ________________ is a great way to get people involved because it affects people's emotions and is fun.

C SPEAK Work in pairs. Do you think viral campaigns are an effective way to raise awareness of an issue? Why/Why not?

VOCABULARY
Adjective + noun collocations

Adjective + noun collocations

Some adjectives and nouns are commonly used together. For example, we say *negative attitude* NOT ~~*negative belief*~~.

Match the numbers (1–6) with the letters (a–f) to form adjective + noun collocations.

1 The number of **online** …
2 There has been a **positive** …
3 One **key** …
4 Hashtags are a great way to raise **public** …
5 Using Twitter allows us to reach a **wider** …
6 The company has made a **substantial** …

a **awareness** of a new campaign.
b **comments** posted is a good measure of success.
c **audience** than through other social media platforms.
d **factor** was the use of social media influencers.
e **reaction** both online and in print media.
f **donation** to the campaign.

PRONUNCIATION
Using intonation to attract and keep interest

10.6 **A Listen to the sentence below being said in two different ways. Check (✓) the one that sounds more engaging.**

By 2014, it had exploded and garnered 1.2 million mentions on social media, with participants in over twenty countries.

☐ Speaker 1 ☐ Speaker 2

B Underline the words you think will be stressed and draw arrows to show where you think the intonation will rise.

1 It's important to show that they aren't alone, that they do have someone to turn to.
2 Just one small donation from you could change the lives of these children forever.
3 It's time we put a stop to this unnecessary suffering. It's time we took a stand.

10.7 **C Listen and check your answers to Exercise B.**

SPEAKING HUB

A PLAN Work in groups of four. You are going to create a viral marketing campaign for a charity or to raise awareness of an issue (e.g. mental health, homelessness, etc). To help you plan, discuss the questions below.

1 Which charity are you going to raise awareness of and try to get regular donations for?
2 How are you going to get more online mentions for your chosen charity?
3 What key factors will hook your audience into the video?
4 Who is going to be your target audience?
5 How are you going to get higher engagement and create viral content?

B PREPARE Film your viral ad.

C PRESENT Play your viral ad to the class. Take a class vote for the ad most likely to go viral.

Report a conversation
Plan and create a viral marketing ad

Café Hub

10.3 Watch on demand

A– *from … to* S– circumlocution

The rise of streaming

COMPREHENSION

A Work in groups. Discuss the questions.

1. Do you prefer streaming movies on platforms like Netflix and Amazon Prime or going to the movie theater?
2. Overall, do you think streaming services have had a positive or negative effect on the movie industry?
3. How do you think movie theaters could adapt to survive the rise of 'on demand' content?

Glossary

influx (n) the arrival of a large amount of people or things at the same time
metric (n) a system or standard for measuring things

B Watch a news report about the rise of video streaming services. Choose the best summary (1 or 2).

1. Streaming services like Netflix have provided a platform for films that might not otherwise have been made.
2. Streaming services like Netflix are now forcing people in the film and TV industry to rethink their approach.

C Watch the report again and answer the questions.

1. According to the presenter, what is usually essential to the success of large film franchises?
2. According to the first interviewee, what won't audiences be able to stream online?
3. Which two examples does the presenter give of cinemas diversifying their business?
4. According to the independent producer, why are many people leaving the film industry to work in TV?

D Work in pairs. Read the extract from the report. What do you think might explain lower ticket sales but higher overall attendance?

Box office sales are no longer the sole metric of success. In fact, so far this year, box office receipts are down, whilst cinema admissions are up.

Glossary

cinema **(n) (British)** = movie theater **(n) (American)**
mum **(n) (British)** = mom **(n) (American)**

AUTHENTIC ENGLISH

A Work in pairs. Read the extract from the report. Why do you think the speaker uses *from … to*? What does this emphasize?

As a result of this revolution, cinemas are changing. They're diversifying to become hubs for community events, **from** live conversation **to** meeting places for new mums.

B Read the information in the box and check your answer to Exercise A.

from … to

In natural spoken English, *from … to* is generally used when talking about the highest and lowest points in a range:

*Subscription packages cost anywhere **from** $22 **to** $65 a month.*

However, it can also be used to make arguments sound more persuasive by giving two very different examples that show how big the range of something is.

*These days, we can stream everything **from** the latest blockbuster movies **to** children's cartoons.*

Although this structure usually follows the main claim or argument, it can also be used to introduce it:

***From** the atmosphere **to** the size of the screen, a movie theater offers a great deal that streaming services simply cannot match.*

C Work in pairs. Take turns completing the sentence prompts with *from … to* and your own ideas.

1. My hometown has a lot to offer, …
2. … , there are many clear benefits of social media.
3. There are a lot of people who could play me in a movie, …
4. There's a lot we can do to tackle climate change, …
5. … , there are a lot of advantages to being self-employed.
6. There are multiple reasons to go vegetarian, …

My hometown has a lot to offer, from world-class theater to excellent burgers and fries.

Some big news

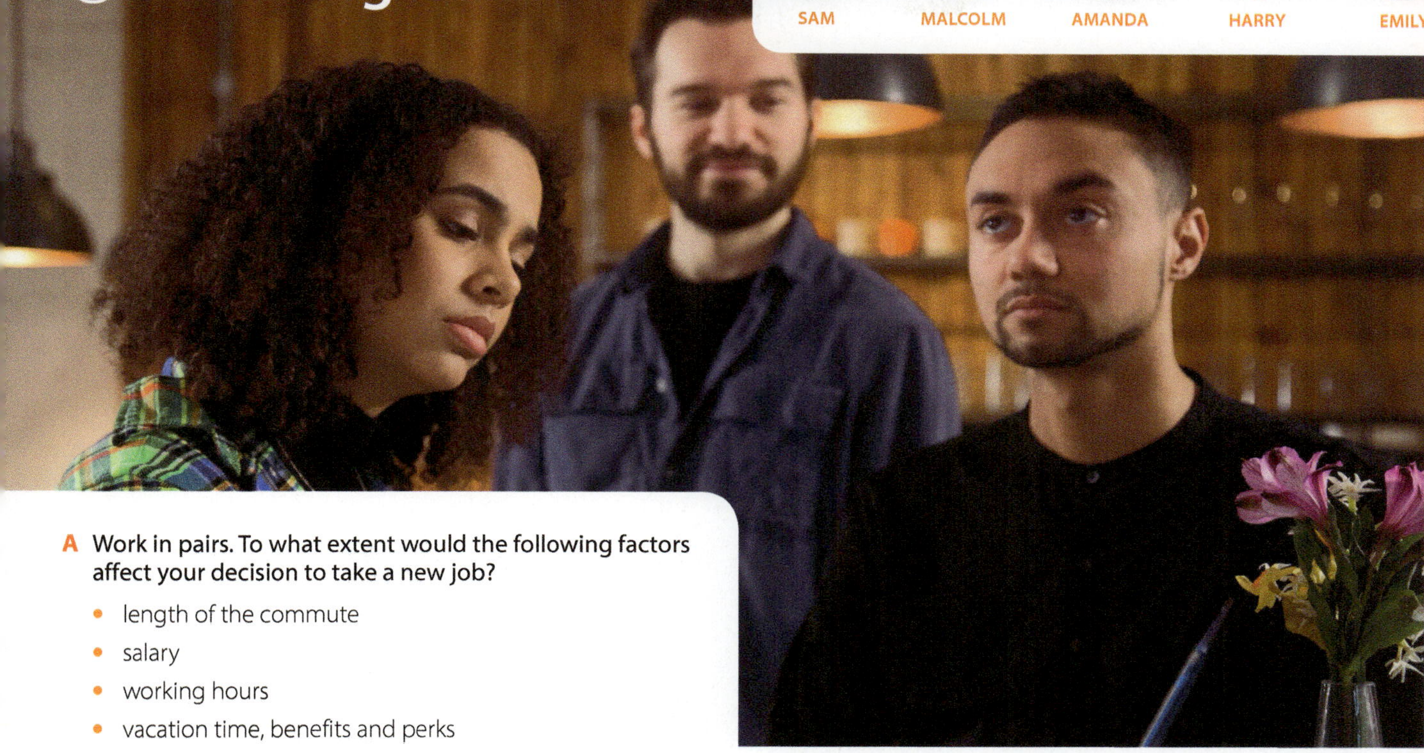

A **Work in pairs. To what extent would the following factors affect your decision to take a new job?**

- length of the commute
- salary
- working hours
- vacation time, benefits and perks

B **Watch the video and answer the questions.**

1 What are the advantages of Amanda's new job?
2 Why do you think she is reluctant to take it?

SPEAKING SKILL

A **Match the extracts (1–3) to their meanings (a–c).**

1 Well, that's certainly not near here.
2 And I know that I certainly wouldn't be disappointed if you decided not to go.
3 I guess I just need to be given a good reason to stay by someone, really.

a I don't want you to go.
b Give me a reason to stay.
c It's really far away.

B **Work in pairs. Are Harry and Amanda being vague or direct? Why?**

C **Read the information in the box and check your answers to Exercise A.**

> **Circumlocution**
>
> Using more words than is necessary when fewer would do is called circumlocution. This is something we do to be vague or evasive, usually because we are embarrassed, uncomfortable or simply want to avoid saying something. Circumlocution is typically signaled by phrases such as: *I guess what I'm trying to say is …, I just kind of want you to know that …, I suppose what I mean is …*

D **Work in pairs. Take turns breaking the bad news below to each other using circumlocution.**

- All the money has been stolen out of their bank account.
- You have spilled coffee on their brand-new white carpet.
- You had said that they could have the day off tomorrow, but now you need them to come in to work.
- You have forgotten to send the important letter that they asked you to mail.
- They are going on vacation tomorrow, but the airline they are flying with has gone out of business.

SPEAKING HUB

A **PREPARE** **Work in pairs. Brainstorm the advantages and disadvantages of video streaming services.**

B **PLAN** **Work in two groups. You are going to debate the following:**

Video streaming services have had a negative impact on the movie and television industry.

Group A – You agree with the idea above.

Group B – You disagree with the idea above.

Plan your arguments. Think about how to support your position, as well as what the other group might say.

C **SPEAK** **Hold your debate.**

Give your opinion on streaming services

➤ Turn to page 163 to learn how to write a persuasive essay.

Unit 10 Review

VOCABULARY

A Complete the text with the correct form of the words in the box.

bias   broadsheet   coverage   editor   headline   tabloid

What your newspaper says about you

The newspaper a person reads says a lot about who they are. In the US and many other countries, 1 ______________ newspapers are traditionally smaller in size and their stories are shorter. The 2 ______________ are usually more shocking and many of the stories focus on people and celebrities. 3 ______________, on the other hand, are usually larger in size and much of the 4 ______________ in these newspapers focuses on serious stories rather than celebrity gossip. In both cases, the paper's 5 ______________ decides what gets published and can have a huge influence on their readers. Many newspapers in the US tend to be 6 ______________ toward one of the two main political parties and people will usually not buy a paper that supports the other party.

B Complete the infographic with the correct form of the words in the box.

campaign   follower   hashtag   influencer   meme   reach   trend   viral

The power of Social Media

- Katy Perry, Justin Bieber and Barack Obama all have over **100 million** 1 ______________ on Twitter.
- 2 ______________ are used **125 million** times a day on Twitter.
- PewDiePie is, without a doubt, one of the **biggest** 3 ______________ on social media, with over **60 million** subscribers to his YouTube channel.
- When a music video goes 4 ______________ it can 5 ______________ **billions** of people. 'Despacito' has had over **5 billion** views.
- A short 6 ______________ is much more likely to be **successful** than a long one.
- A social media marketing 7 ______________ is a cheap and quick way to reach **millions** of people.
- 'Stranger Things' was the **highest** 8 ______________ search for a TV show on Google in 2017.

C Choose the correct options to complete the sentences.

1 Celebrity endorsement is a great way to raise public ***awareness* / *understanding*** of a campaign.
2 Going viral was a ***key* / *main*** factor in the charity's success.
3 The charity has received a lot of positive online ***posts* / *comments*** recently.
4 Overall, we've had a pretty ***positive* / *affirmative*** reaction from the public.
5 The actress made a ***consequential* / *substantial*** donation to charity.
6 In order to reach a ***wider* / *deeper*** audience, you need a good hashtag.
7 We need to carry out a ***thorough* / *deep*** investigation into why this campaign failed.
8 I don't understand why there was such a ***negative* / *poor*** reaction to our ad.

GRAMMAR

A Rewrite the sentences in reported speech.

1 'I've been working every night this week.'
Nicki said ______________.
2 'I'm going to be about ten minutes late.'
Jonas says ______________.
3 'Have you always wanted to go to college?'
He asked ______________.
4 'We were trying to find somewhere to park.'
She said ______________.
5 'I'll let you know when I'm finished.'
Marco said ______________.
6 'I'd wanted to tell her for months.'
Alex said ______________.
7 'I will need some help with my project.'
Pablo says ______________.
8 'Where can I find a good seafood restaurant?'
Sofia asked ______________.

B Are these sentences correct or incorrect? Rewrite the incorrect sentences.

1 Piotr agreed coming to the meeting.
2 She refused to apologize for being late.
3 Maria offered working this weekend.
4 They insisted on to pay for dinner.
5 He congratulated her on passing the exam.
6 She reminded me sending the email.
7 They invited us having dinner with them.
8 They advised me to get there fifteen minutes early.

Endmatter Contents

Grammar Hub

Vocabulary Hub

Communication Hub

Writing

Grammar Hub

6.1 Obligation, prohibition and permission

Strong obligation

- We use *have to*, *must*, *need to*, *be obliged to* and *be required to* to talk about things that we are obligated to do / are necessary.

  The meeting starts at 9:00 am, so you must be here before then.
  (= It's necessary for you to be here before 9:00 am.)
  You need to buy a ticket before boarding.
  (= It's necessary to buy a ticket.)

Lack of obligation

- We use *don't have to*, *don't need to*, *be not obliged to* and *be not required to* to talk about things that we aren't obligated to do / aren't necessary.

  The dress code is semi-formal, but staff members aren't required to wear ties. (= They can wear ties if they want to, but it's not necessary.)

Be careful!

- We cannot use *must not* in this way.

  They don't have to study music if they don't want to. NOT ~~*They must not study music if they don't want to.*~~

Weak obligation

- We use *should* to talk about things that are advised, recommended or suggested, but aren't necessary.

  You should read the report before our meeting with Alex tomorrow. (= It isn't necessary to read the report, but it's a good idea.)

- We use *be supposed to* to talk about things we're expected to do according to a rule or arrangement.

  I'm supposed to go to that meeting at 2:00 pm, but I really don't want to!

Prohibition

- We use *must not*, *can't* and *be not allowed to* to talk about things that are prohibited / not permitted.

  You can't smoke anywhere inside the building. (= You're not permitted to smoke.)

6.2 Articles

- We use the indefinite article (*a/an*):

  a when we talk about something for the first time.
  *My sister-in-law just bought **a** new car.*

  b when it's not clear or important which exact thing is being talked about (e.g. when something is one of many).
  *I'm going to **a study group** later with **a friend**.*
  *I actually read **a really interesting book** about entrepreneurs.*

- We use the definite article (*the*):

  a when there's only one of something.
  *Sorry, could you close **the door**? (= There's only one door in the room.)*

  b when it's clear to both speaker and listener which specific thing is being talked about.
  *What do you think of **the new science teacher**?*

  c with superlatives.
  *Jupiter is **the biggest** planet in the solar system.*

  d with rivers, some mountains, oceans, seas, plural country names, groups of islands and deserts.
  *Amazingly, he managed to land on **the Hudson River**.*

- We use no article:

  a to talk about things in general.
  More money needs to be spent on education in this country.

  b with most towns, cities, countries, continents, states, lakes and mountains.
  *Yale is an American university in **New Haven**, Connecticut.*

6.1 Obligation, prohibition and permission

A **Complete the conversations with the correct form of the words and phrases in the box.**

be required to	be supposed to	
have to	must not	not need to

1 **A:** You ________________ tell anyone that I'm here. I want it to be a surprise!
B: OK, I promise!

2 **A:** ________________ visitors legally ________________ wear helmets?
B: Absolutely! It's far too dangerous not to.

3 **A:** What do you ________________ get in town today?
B: A new suit for my job interview next week.

4 **A:** Do you want to play tennis tomorrow?
B: No, I can't. I ________________ not ________________ put pressure on my wrist until it heals properly.

5 **A:** Should we plan to get to the airport at two?
B: We ________________ get there so early. Three should be fine.

B **Complete the second sentence so it has a similar meaning to the first using the words in bold.**

1 Booking our flights soon is probably a good idea. **should**
I think ________________________________ our flights soon.

2 A high level of English is essential for all applicants. **obliged**
All applicants ________________________________ a high level of English.

3 My parents said I could stay up to watch the final. **let**
My parents ________________________________ stay up to watch the final.

4 I don't know why they didn't let us take our bikes on the train. **allowed**
I don't know why we ________________________________ take our bikes on the train.

5 Taking food and drink into the library isn't permitted. **can't**
You ________________________________ food and drink into the library.

6 It's your choice whether you come with us. **have**
If you don't want to, you ________________________________ come with us.

➤ Go back to page 63.

6.2 Articles

A **Choose the correct articles to complete the sentences.**

1 How long have you lived in *a* / *the* / – US, Misha?
2 I saw *an* / *the* / – amazing documentary on Netflix last night.
3 For their wedding anniversary this year, my parents are going to *a* / *the* / – Paris.
4 What do you think of *a* / *the* / – new sound equipment in the lecture hall?
5 My roommate Idris is a nurse at *an* / *the* / – hospital on Jones Street.
6 It's not a bad idea to do away with *a* / *the* / – meat in your diet.
7 This is by far *a* / *the* / – worst food I've ever eaten!
8 My dad's school wasn't in New York City; it was in *a* / *the* / – small town out in the country.

B **Complete the sentences with *a*, *an*, *the* or – (no article).**

1 Seeing kids in school uniforms is ___ unusual sight around here.
2 Lizzie, just do your best on ___ exam tomorrow – that's all you can do.
3 Imagine riding a camel in the burning heat of ___ Sahara Desert.
4 I've never been to ___ job interview before.
5 One thing I could never do without is ___ books.
6 How cold does it get in ___ Antarctica in the winter?
7 I was really excited to see that ___ book Sean gave me for my birthday is signed by the author.
8 How old were you when you first went to ___ college?

C **Are these sentences correct or incorrect? Rewrite the incorrect sentences.**

1 Lina will be waiting for us once we get off a bus.
2 Aisha got accepted by the university in the US – in California, I believe.
3 It was a successful meeting despite all the interruptions.
4 The Houses of Parliament in London are right next to the River Thames.
5 An exercise is always hard, but it's worth it if you value your health.
6 Most people these days have the smartphone, don't they?
7 Fran is very good at finding the bargains.
8 I'm simply too scared to try a bungee jumping.

➤ Go back to page 67.

Grammar Hub

7.1 First conditional with different future forms; Unreal conditionals

First conditional

- We use the first conditional (*if* + present + future) to talk about something that will probably happen in the future.
- We can use any present tense in the *if* clause (e.g. simple present, present progressive, present perfect, etc) and any future form in the main clause (e.g. *will*, *be going to*, future progressive, etc).

  If the weather improves, we're going to hold the event outside.

  If you're staying in tonight, I'll order us a pizza.

  They're going to let us know if their train is delayed.

  I'll be amazed if we've finished the meeting by three o'clock.
- We can also use an imperative in the main clause.

  Come and meet us later if you finish early.

Be careful!

- We can put the *if* clause or the result clause first. The only difference is we do not use a comma if we begin with the result clause.

  If the weather's nice tomorrow, we'll go to the beach.

  We'll go to the beach tomorrow if the weather's nice.

Unreal conditionals

Second conditional

- We use the second conditional (*if* + simple past + *would/might/could* + base form) to talk about imaginary or hypothetical situations in the present or future and their consequences.

  If I had enough money, I'd open a restaurant.
  (= I don't have enough money; I'm just imagining.)

  We couldn't order things online if credit and debit cards didn't exist. (= This is hypothetical, because credit and debit cards do exist.)

Third conditional

- We use the third conditional (*if* + past perfect + *would/could/might have* + past participle) to talk about a hypothetical situation in the past and its consequences.

  If I had known about the event, I'd definitely have gone to it. (= I didn't know about the event so I didn't go to it.)

Mixed conditionals

- We can also use a mixture of second and third conditionals (*if* + past perfect + *would/might/could* + base form) to talk about a hypothetical past situation with a present result.

  If you'd spent more time studying, you wouldn't be so nervous now.

7.2 *wish* and *if only*

- We use *wish* + simple past to talk about things we would like to be different in the present or future, but are impossible or unlikely to change.

  I wish my brother lived closer to Chicago. (= This is unlikely to change – I'm just imagining.)

  I wish I could speak Japanese. (= This is unlikely to change soon – I'm just imagining.)
- We use *wish* + past perfect to talk about things we regret in the past.

  I wish I'd told Yuko how I felt before she moved back to Japan. (= but I didn't tell her)

  I feel sick! I wish I hadn't eaten so much at lunchtime! (= but I did eat too much)
- We use *wish* + object + *would* + base form to talk about things we want to happen or stop happening in the present, usually because they annoy us.

  I wish you'd stop talking with your mouth full – it's disgusting!

  I wish people wouldn't just throw their garbage in the street.
- We can use *if only* instead of *wish* in all of the structures above to sound more dramatic/ emphatic.

  If only I'd paid more attention in school!
- We can use *were* instead of *was* after *I/he/she/it* in the *if* clause.

  I wish I was/were a little bit taller.
  (= This is impossible – I'm just imagining.)

Be careful!

- When you want to make a wish about yourself, or you and other people, use *could* instead of *would*.

  I wish I could sit at home all day. NOT ~~*I wish I would sit at home all day.*~~

7.1 First conditional with different future forms

Correct the mistakes in the sentences.

1 Let me know if you'll need any help with anything.
2 We're going to miss the beginning if we won't leave soon.
3 If everything goes well, we'll have been finishing by Friday.
4 Could I borrow that book if you won't be using it?
5 Don't go to work if you won't be feeling well.
6 If I'll get a bonus this year, I'm going to go to Hawaii.
7 I'll have let you know if I think I'm going to be late.
8 If you'll have been there before, you'll know how busy it gets.

➤ Go back to page 75.

Unreal conditionals

A Choose the correct options to complete the conditional sentences.

1 If you found a better job, you ***can*** / ***could*** start saving some money.
2 Ellie would prefer it if she ***didn't have*** / ***hadn't had*** to share a room.
3 ***We'll*** / ***We'd*** have been waiting for hours if you hadn't stopped to give us a ride.
4 If the car had gone over the cliff, we wouldn't ***get*** / ***have gotten*** out alive.
5 I'd join a gym if I ***wasn't*** / ***hadn't been*** so lazy!
6 If she ***saw*** / ***'d seen*** me, she'd have waved.
7 You ***won't*** / ***wouldn't*** be standing here talking to me now if you'd actually won the lottery.
8 If I'd entered the competition, I'm sure ***I'd*** / ***I'll*** have done better than Mo did.

B Complete the profile with the correct form of the verbs in the box. Add modal verbs where appropriate.

attract be can do still have succeed turn out

Business profile: Sean Taylor / the restaurant *Pie*

Sean no longer has *Pie*, the restaurant in Orlando, Florida he opened two years ago, but says that if he [1] ________________ things differently in the past, maybe he [2] ________________ it today. The first mistake Sean made was to prepare the food himself. If he'd employed a chef, maybe it [3] ________________ better for the business. Sean says that if he [4] ________________ , he would go back in time and spend more time running the restaurant. He strongly believes the business [5] ________________ if he'd spent more time with his customers. Second, he didn't promote and market it effectively. If he had done that, he [6] ________________ more diners. Third, if he had tried to sell the restaurant rather than just closing it, he [7] ________________ in the poor financial situation he's in now.

➤ Go back to page 77.

7.2 *wish* and *if only*

A Complete the sentences with the correct form of the verb in parentheses. Use contractions where possible.

1 I've been dreaming about getting a new car. If only I ________________ (*have*) enough money!
2 I sent an email to the wrong person today. I wish I ________________ (*not make*) such a silly mistake.
3 You really should ________________ (*buy*) that cheap laptop when you had the opportunity.
4 I wish you ________________ (*stop*) doing that – it's so annoying!
5 I love my job. If only I ________________ (*not have to*) work weekends!
6 I wish I ________________ (*can*) go with you tomorrow!
7 If only my grades ________________ (*be*) better. Then I would have gone to college, but it's too late now.
8 I wonder where Patrícia is now. I wish I ________________ (*ask*) her out all those years ago.

B Correct the mistakes in the sentences.

1 If only I've spent more time studying when I was a student.
2 I wish I didn't miss out on that opportunity to teach at a summer camp last year.
3 I find it hard to meet people. If only I'm not so painfully shy.
4 You're really hard to talk to today. I wish you hadn't been in such a bad mood.
5 I wish I would move back to where I grew up but I can't afford a house there.
6 I wish he had stop thinking about himself.
7 I really wish we had moved here – it was a big mistake.
8 You shouldn't tell Mei Xing that you were leaving. Now she's upset.

➤ Go back to page 79.

8.1 Past modals of deduction

- We use *must have* + past participle to say that we are almost sure that something happened or was true.

  She's pale and her hands are shaking – she must have had a substantial shock. (= I'm sure she had a shock.)
  Being alone on a mountain all night must have been terrifying! (= I'm sure it was terrifying.)
- We use *can't have* + past participle to say that we are almost sure something didn't happen or wasn't true.

  It can't have been easy living in such an isolated village. (= I'm sure it wasn't easy.)
- We use *may/might/could have* + past participle to say that we think it's possible that something happened or was true.

  Héctor isn't here yet – he may/might/could have gotten stuck in traffic.
  (= It's possible he got stuck in traffic.)
- We use *may/might* + *not* + *have* + past participle to say that we think it's possible that something hasn't happened but we are not certain.

  I'll call Agnes because she may/might not have heard the news yet.
  (= It's possible she hasn't heard the news yet.)

Be careful!

- *Could have* means that something possibly happened in the past, but *couldn't have* means we are certain that something did not happen.

  You could have left your phone at the office. (= It is possible.)
  You couldn't have left your phone at the office, because you just called me. (= It's impossible.)

8.2 Order of adjectives

- When we use two or more adjectives before a noun, we usually put the adjectives in the following order:

Opinion	Size	Age	Shape	Color	Origin	Material
beautiful	huge	20th century	rectangular	blue	English	leather
great	long	ancient	round	green	Italian	silk
old-fashioned	tiny	up-to-date	square	white	Turkish	wooden

Monika bought a stunning old crystal vase. (= opinion → age → material)
We got some big heart-shaped gold balloons for the party. (= size → shape → color)
Rapini is a delicious green Italian vegetable. (= opinion → color → origin)

- Opinion adjectives (e.g. *unusual*, *disgusting*, etc) are always used before descriptive adjectives (e.g. *enormous*, *circular*, etc).

  He was wearing a disgusting pink silk shirt. NOT ~~He was wearing a pink silk disgusting shirt.~~
  They found a beautiful ancient golden crown. NOT ~~They found an ancient golden beautiful crown.~~
- We usually use *and* between two or more adjectives of the same type, especially with colors.

  He showed me an old black and white photograph of his family.
  I love Portugal's beautiful blue and white tiles.

Be careful!

- Although not grammatically incorrect, it's very unusual for a description to use more than three adjectives, so it's better to avoid this.

  She was sitting at a beautiful, long, modern, square table.

- Compound adjectives (e.g. *long-term*, *state-of-the-art*, etc) should also be used in this order.

  She bought a great state-of-the art computer.

8.1 Past modals of deduction

A Choose the correct options to complete the sentences.

1 They're more than an hour late. They *must have* / *can't have* gotten lost.
2 Patrick *can't have* / *could have* gone to the opera. He hates classical music!
3 You passed! You *might have* / *must have* been so happy when you heard the results!
4 It *must have* / *can't have* been food poisoning. Nobody else who ate the fish got sick.
5 You *can't have* / *might not have* seen Marco in town. He's on vacation in Spain right now.
6 Sasha *couldn't have* / *might not have* heard the news yet, so let's call her just in case.
7 I *must have* / *can't have* left my bank card at the café – I used it just now to pay for the coffee.
8 He hasn't answered his phone for two days. I suppose he *may have* / *can't have* lost it.
9 I *can't have* / *must have* left my hat at the restaurant. That's the last place I had it.
10 It's not very likely because she's 103, but I suppose it *can't have* / *might have* been Grandma you saw at the grocery store.

B Complete the conversations with a modal verb and the correct form of the verbs in the box.

be do finish land make see

1 **A:** Here's that report you asked for.
B: You ________________ already! You only started it yesterday.
2 **A:** $20 for two cups of coffee!
B: That can't be right. The waiter ________________ ________________ a mistake.
3 **A:** Did the children break the baby's toy?
B: They ________________ it. They were at school all day.
4 **A:** Do you think Kobi's still on the plane?
B: Uh, he ________________ by now. It depends if there was a delay or not.
5 **A:** I can't imagine what Julie went through when she lost her father.
B: Yes, it ________________ awful for her.
6 **A:** It's strange that Doug hasn't replied to my email.
B: He ________________ it yet. He doesn't always check his email on the weekend.

➤ Go back to page 87.

8.2 Order of adjectives

A Add the adjectives in bold in the correct place in each sentence.

1 So, apparently, Saga used to have long hair. **blond**
2 What a silver bracelet that is! **beautiful**
3 The rupee is a small Indian coin. **round**
4 We now have four delightful puppies to take care of. **tiny**
5 There are some huge ancient statues in the museum. **bronze**
6 She gently held the strange rectangular box in her hand. **wooden**
7 If it's a stunning pink flower, it's probably a lotus. **bright**
8 'What is this peculiar yellow fruit?' he wondered. **oval**
9 I have no idea what this odd-looking metal instrument was used for. **circular**
10 When I was younger, I had a green and red jacket that I wore almost every day. **ridiculous**
11 My brother got a new job at the hospital. **part-time**
12 They presented a comprehensive plan. **long-term**

B Correct five mistakes with the order of adjectives in the extract.

There was silence, except for the regular ticking of the Victorian tall grandfather clock in the hallway. Noah and Emily stood at the bottom of the wooden steep staircase, looking up into the darkness. Noah turned on his flashlight. Its strong bright beam lit up the wall. Hanging just above their heads was a painting – the medieval priceless portrait of Anne of Avalon which they had been searching for for so long.

As they stared at the picture, Emily felt something brush against her leg. 'What was that?' she said. Noah swung the flashlight around. By the large ancient stone fireplace was an old black and white cat, staring at them. Hanging from the cat's collar was a rusty strange-looking small key. 'I wonder if that key opens the old metal box we found in the kitchen,' said Emily.

'I was just thinking the same thing,' Noah replied.

➤ Go back to page 91.

Grammar Hub

9.1 Adjective clauses

Types of adjective clause

- We use essential adjective clauses to identify exactly which person or thing we are talking about.

  The woman who sits next to me at work is studying for an MA in her free time.

- We use non-essential adjective clauses to give extra, non-essential information about a person or thing. We use commas to separate this clause from the rest of the sentence.

  The band, whose debut album was released in 1991, has sold over 32 million records in the US alone. (= We don't need to know when their debut album was released – this is just extra information.)

Relative pronouns

- All adjective clauses begin with a relative pronoun. We use *who* for people, *which* for things, *where* for places, *when* for times and *whose* for possession.

  Apparently, the store where I bought my computer closed down recently.

  Sam, whose mom owns a business, wants to open his own store.

- In essential adjective clauses:

  a we can use *that* instead of *who* or *which*.

  We're really looking for someone who/that has experience teaching children.

  b we can omit *who*, *that* and *which* when they are the object of the adjective clause.

  The employee (that) we spoke to wasn't very helpful.

  c we can never omit *where* or *whose*.

  My parents have just sold the house where I grew up. NOT ~~*My parents have just sold the house I grew up.*~~

- In non-essential adjective clauses:

  a we cannot use *that* instead of *who* or *which*.

  My sister, who recently graduated from Harvard, just got a new job. NOT ~~*My sister, that recently graduated from Harvard, just got a new job.*~~

  b we cannot omit the relative pronoun.

  Michael Jackson, who died in 2009, was known as the 'King of Pop'. NOT ~~*Michael Jackson, died in 2009, was known as the 'King of Pop'.*~~

9.2 Determiners and quantifiers

few, much, many, a little, etc

- We use *(too) many*, *few*, *a few*, *several*, *a large number of* and *hundreds/thousands of* with countable nouns.

  Not many people can afford to buy designer clothes.

  There are hundreds of bargains to choose from.

- We use *(too) much*, *a little*, *little*, *a great deal of* and *a large amount of* with uncountable nouns.

  We spend a great deal of money on things we don't need!

- We can use *a lot of*, *lots of*, *plenty of*, *enough*, *some* and *any* with both countable and uncountable nouns.

  Plenty of successful people never went to college.

  Did I put enough milk in your coffee?

all, each, every

- We use *all*, *all the*, *all of the* with plural nouns to talk about every person or thing in a group.

  All participants were asked to complete an online survey about their phobias.

- We use *each* and *every* with singular nouns to talk about all of the people or things in a group when considered separately.

  Each competitor was given a medal for taking part.

both, either, neither

- We use *both* with plural nouns to talk about two people or things. *Both* or *both of* can be used before a determiner (e.g. *the*, *my*, *those*, etc), but we always use *both of* before pronouns (e.g. *her*, *their*, *its*, etc).

  Both restaurants offer a range of vegetarian options.

- We use *either* (… *or*) with singular nouns to talk about one of two people or things when it's not important which, or to mean *both*.

  Which color do you prefer? I'm happy with either.

- We use *neither* (… *nor*) with singular nouns to mean *not either* of two people or things.

  Neither side played very well in the last game.

- We use *either of* / *neither of* with plural pronouns or plural nouns with determiners.

  Neither of them could decide which car to buy.

no, none, any

- We use *no* or *none* in positive sentences and *any* in negative sentences to refer to zero quantity.

  It seems there are no tickets left for tonight's show.

Be careful!

- *Few* is negative, and means *not many*. *A few* is positive and means *some, but not many*.
- Similarly, *little* is negative, and means *not much*. *A little* is positive and means *some, but not much*.

9.1 Adjective clauses

A Choose the correct options to complete the sentences.

1 Last summer, I visited my cousin, ***who*** / ***whose*** lives in a nice apartment in New York.
2 There's the new store **–** / ***where*** I was telling you about.
3 The recruiter ***who*** / ***which*** helped is my cousin, Léo.
4 The woman ***whose*** / ***who*** house we stayed in had listed it on Airbnb.
5 It's usually late at night ***where*** / ***when*** I feel hungriest.
6 My car, ***that*** / ***which*** I've had since May, uses a lot of gas.
7 Thanks, Fiona. The recommendation **–** / ***who*** you gave me was a great idea.
8 The house ***which*** / ***in which*** I grew up is now a hotel.

B Combine the sentences using an adjective clause. Omit the relative pronoun where possible.

1 San Francisco is where the company was founded. It is also home to TechCorp.
San Francisco ______________________________.
2 I used to work in a call center. It's just gone out of business.
The call center ______________________________.
3 Mark Allen created the app in his bedroom. He is now worth $20 billion.
Mark Allen ______________________________.
4 Sadly it was no longer under warranty. This means I can't get my money back.
Sadly ______________________________.
5 The app allows users to order food 24 hours a day. It has received mixed reviews.
The app ______________________________.
6 I sit next to a woman at work who has a degree in customer service management.
The woman ______________________________.

C Are these sentences correct or incorrect? Rewrite the incorrect sentences.

1 My company that is based in New York has offices all over the world.
2 The slight problem, that you told me about, can't easily be fixed.
3 The movies that are playing at that movie theater are never very good.
4 My coffee maker, I paid a lot for, makes terrible coffee!
5 Where's the complaint form the customer filled out?
6 The customer called about the problem is still on the phone.
7 The woman, whose tablet I was borrowing, just told me to keep it!
8 The store I got bad service from which isn't getting my business anymore!

➤ Go back to page 99.

9.2 Determiners and quantifiers

A Choose the correct options to complete the sentences.

1 I know ***a little*** / ***a few*** brands in this store.
2 There isn't ***much*** / ***many*** information on this label.
3 ***A large amount*** / ***A large number*** of products were recalled.
4 ***Neither*** / ***Both*** the seller and the buyer are concerned about prices.
5 ***Either*** / ***Neither*** you exchange it or issue a refund!
6 ***A few*** / ***A little*** of the customers complained.
7 Sadly, there are ***none*** / ***no*** left.
8 ***All*** / ***Each*** products must be returned with a receipt.

B Choose the correct option (a, b or c) to complete the sentences.

1 Contrary to popular belief, ___ people make purchases based on online reviews.
a much **b** neither **c** few
2 It's important that you include at least ___ vegetables in your diet if you want to stay healthy.
a few **b** both **c** a few
3 ___ food bloggers have become very important because they can influence food trends.
a Plenty of **b** Much **c** Every
4 ___ food companies make health claims about their products to encourage consumers to buy them.
a Both **b** Neither **c** Either
5 Drinking a large ___ of coffee does not actually dehydrate you.
a amount **b** plenty **c** number
6 Drinking ___ coffee may help to improve your concentration, but don't drink too much.
a a little **b** little **c** plenty
7 ___ product was successful because they were considered to be too unhealthy.
a Both **b** Neither **c** Either
8 ___ of the products turned out to be healthy as they claimed to be.
a No **b** None **c** Any

➤ Go back to page 103.

Grammar Hub

10.1 Reported speech

- When we report what someone said, we usually change the main verb by moving it back one tense into the past.

Direct speech	Reported speech
simple present '**I'm** completely exhausted.'	simple past She said (that) **she was** completely exhausted.
present progressive '**We're trying** to find a solution.'	past progressive They said (that) **they were trying** to find a solution.
simple past '**Online hits went** up.'	past perfect He said (that) **online hits had gone** up.
past progressive '**We were finding** it hard.'	past perfect progressive She said (that) **they had been finding** it hard.
present perfect '**I've made** a decision.'	past perfect He said **he'd made** a decision.
present perfect progressive '**I've been working**.'	past perfect progressive She said (that) **she had been working**.
will/can/may '**I'll let** you know tomorrow.' '**I can double-check** for you.' '**You may need** to book early.'	*would/could/might* He said (that) **he'd let** me know the next day. She said (that) **she could double-check** for me. She said (that) **we might need** to book early.

- We don't need to change the tense in reported speech:
  - **a** when the direct speech is in the past perfect (simple or progressive).
    'We had wanted to move for some time.' → He said they had wanted to move for some time.
  - **b** with the modal verbs *could, should, would, might* and *need*.
    'You might be able to get some money back.' → He said that we might be able to get some money back.
    'You don't need to worry.' → She said that I don't need to worry.
  - **c** when the information is still true or relevant, or the reporting verb is in the present tense.
    'My sister lives in Japan.' → She told me that her sister lives in Japan. (= It's still true that her sister lives there.)
- We usually do need to change time references, pronouns, etc.
  'See you tomorrow.' → She told me that she would see me the next day.

Reported questions

- When we report questions, the tense of the main verb changes but we don't use the auxiliary verb *do*. We also use the same word order as a positive sentence.
  'Where did you grow up?' → She asked me where I had grown up.
  NOT ~~She asked me where did I grow up.~~
- When we report yes/no questions we use *if* or *whether*.
  'Did you enjoy it?' → She asked me if I had enjoyed it.
  'Does she usually finish at 4 pm?' → He asked me whether she usually finishes at 4 pm.

10.2 Reporting verbs

- As well as *say* or *tell*, we can also use other reporting verbs (e.g. *threaten, promise, warn*, etc) to help summarize the meaning of what was said, to describe the speaker's attitude, or to indicate our stance.
  'I'm sorry I'm late.' → She apologized for being late.
- Reporting verbs are followed by a range of different structures:
  - **a** *argue, claim, confirm, decide, recommend, state, suggest*, etc + (*that*) + clause.
    He claimed that he was innocent.
    The police stated that they have made an arrest.
  - **b** *assure, inform, promise, remind*, etc + object + (*that*) + clause.
    Sarah assured me that she would pay me back.
    She promised him that it would never happen again.
  - **c** *decide, promise, refuse, threaten*, etc + the infinitive.
    She refused to tell me why I had been unsuccessful.
    Neighbors threated to call the police.
  - **d** *advise, ask, convince, encourage, persuade, remind, warn*, etc + object + the infinitive.
    My wife encouraged me to apply for the position.
  - **e** *accuse (sb) of, admit, apologize (to sb) for, blame (sb) for, confess to, insist on, recommend, regret, report, suggest*, etc + verb + *-ing*.
    She insisted on paying for the meal.
- Some reporting verbs, such as *persuade, warn, tell* and *ask*, can be followed by a negative infinitive.
  They persuaded her not to say anything at the press conference.

10.1 Reported speech

A Complete the second sentence so it has a similar meaning to the first.

1 'I've been working here for almost six months.'
Francis said that she ______________________
at the company for almost six months.

2 'I'm going to be a little late for the meeting.'
Andy says he ______________________
a little late for the meeting.

3 'Can I have a quick word with you, please, Mr. Jenkins?'
Susie asked me if she ______________________
______________________ a quick word with me.

4 'I'd been hoping you'd have found a solution by now.'
Their boss said he ______________________
we would have found a solution by then.

5 'What time did you get home from work yesterday, Sofia?'
He asked me what time I ______________________
______________________ home from work the day before.

6 'I think I know someone who might be able to fix this.'
Thais said she ______________________
someone who might be able to fix the problem.

7 'I'll call you around seven o'clock.'
Lars told me that he ______________________
me around seven o'clock.

8 'We were driving around for a long time before we found a place to park.'
Mom said they ______________________
around for a long time before they found a place to park.

B Rewrite the sentences and questions in reported speech. Add any information necessary.

1 'I'm not interested in hearing your excuses.'
Olga told me ______________________.

2 'In the end, the event was a big success.'
Juan said that, in the end, ______________________.

3 'Do you want to meet for coffee after work?'
She asked me ______________________.

4 'I've decided I am going to move to a new house soon.'
Jonas said ______________________.

5 'What are you planning to do about your noisy neighbors?'
Daryl asked me ______________________.

6 'Can you play somewhere else? I'm trying to work!'
Mom asked the kids ______________________.

7 'Hi Mateo! I was looking for you yesterday.'
Renata told me that ______________________.

8 'I've been working on a secret project.'
He said ______________________.

➤ Go back to page 111.

10.2 Reporting verbs

A Complete the news story with the reporting verbs in the box.

apologized assured blamed confirmed
decided insisted refused stated

XPS TO CLOSE ITS LONDON OFFICE AFTER 50 YEARS

In an announcement yesterday afternoon, Michael Winters, CEO of XPS, [1] ______________ rumors that the company would be closing its London offices after almost half a century in the capital. After talking about how important the site had been to the company, Winters [2] ______________ on reminding reporters that XPS was still one of the most profitable businesses in its sector. He said that the board had only [3] ______________ to do it because there was no alternative, and [4] ______________ the economy for falling sales. Winters [5] ______________ to the staff for causing them anxiety about the future but he [6] ______________ them that they would be offered jobs in different locations. He [7] ______________ to comment on whether more offices were going to be closed and [8] ______________ that he would give further information when it was available.

B Are these sentences correct or incorrect? Rewrite the incorrect sentences.

1 A confidential source revealed that the company had lost $10 billion.
2 The police refused comment on an open investigation.
3 She threatened calling the police if they didn't leave immediately.
4 His lawyers advised him not to publish the story until after the hearing.
5 They assured that his name wouldn't be mentioned in the article.
6 Under pressure, she admitted fabricating the entire story.
7 The company accused Ms. Hartmann with leaking information to the press.
8 In court, Mr. Petrov confessed to willingly mislead the public.

➤ Go back to page 115.

Vocabulary Hub

6.1 Education

Complete the sentences with words from the box.

campus elementary schools entrance exam graduate high schools lectures scholarship seminar vocational

1 The ________________ for All Souls College at Oxford University has been called the world's hardest test. It is impossible to study for because there are no right or wrong answers and the questions are very abstract. The prize is a seven-year ________________!

2 The Open University is designed for distance-learning students. Those who attend can watch ________________ online and write notes. They can also join in smaller online ________________ groups, where they can discuss ideas.

3 In American ________________, students take a traditional academic path. However, in college they can choose a ________________ path that leads to professions such as an electrician or beautician.

4 In China, there is a ________________ of the University of Nottingham. Some of the buildings are identical to the ones on the UK site. Students here ________________ with a University of Nottingham degree.

5 Some five to eleven-year-olds in Bangladesh study in ________________ on boats due to frequent flooding in the country.

➤ Go back to page 64.

7.2 Three-part phrasal verbs

A Match the words in bold to the definitions.

1 I can't **keep up with** all of the technological changes.
2 I think people need to **stand up for** the things they believe in.
3 We seem to **run out of** money every month. We can only just afford our rent!
4 We **teamed up with** a local company to design the gallery.
5 The event lets me **catch up with** old friends.
6 The shelter **takes care of** homeless people in the city.

a to not have any more of something
b to work together
c to continue to learn about something or find out about something
d to find out someone's news
e to look after someone or something
f to defend someone or something that is being criticized or attacked

B Complete the sentences with the correct form of the phrasal verbs in Exercise A.

1 We wanted to ________________ the rights of young people in the community.
2 The plans keep changing so frequently that it's hard to ________________ what is happening.
3 We have ________________ local cafés to provide free food for the homeless.
4 Giving people a more beautiful environment encourages them to ________________ it.
5 A street party is a great way to ________________ neighbors you haven't seen in a while.
6 Our project ________________ government funding, so we crowdsourced the rest of the money needed.

➤ Go back to page 80.

8.2 Crime

Complete the sentences with the correct form of the words in the box.

arrest catch charge commit innocent investigate punishment question sentence witness

1 The police ________________ him for two hours and then ________________ him with identity theft.
2 She claimed to be ________________ but three separate ________________ identified her as being responsible for the crime.
3 He was ________________ with people's credit card details on his computer and was ________________ for credit card fraud. After they ________________ further, he was taken to court, where the judge ________________ him to six years in prison.
4 Some people argue that imprisonment isn't the best ________________ for someone who ________________ a crime, because many go on to reoffend when released.

➤ Go back to page 92.

10.2 Social media

Match the words in bold (1–5) to the definitions (a–f).

1 I was trying to do some online research, but I kept on getting distracted by all the **clickbait** stories.
2 You will need to go further back in that **thread** to find the message about the changes to the schedule.
3 I used to enjoy social media until a **troll** started writing horrible comments on my posts.
4 I think everyone has seen that **meme** of the president dancing – it's hilarious.
5 Why don't you **DM** me so we can discuss this some more?
6 I think that message goes against **netiquette** – it's really aggressive.

a the polite way of expressing yourself or communicating with other people when you are using the internet
b to send a direct message to someone on the microblogging service Twitter
c a link on a website that is designed to catch people's attention and encourage them to read on
d a series of email messages or messages on a forum about a particular subject
e someone who writes negative and hostile comments on a website in order to provoke people
f an image, video or piece of text that spreads very quickly on the internet, typically one which people create different funny versions of

➤ Go back to page 116.

Communication Hub

8.2 Groups

Read the profiles and answer the questions for each suspect. Underline the part of the text that gives you the answers.

1 Where were they at the time of the murder?
2 Why might they have committed the murder?
3 What is their alibi and does anyone else confirm it?

MAGNUS BALDURSSON

- Swedish billionaire oil tycoon
- Mild-mannered, yet a ruthless businessman
- Hates family secrets getting out and works hard to ensure nothing is made public

ALIBI

'What an awful night! I told Sofia that she would be taking over the business when I retire and my son, Linus, was furious. He started shouting about how much debt Sofia was in – apparently she owed over a million dollars to some pretty bad people. Anyway, that's when Sofia ran out in tears. Linus said he was going to his room, but when I went to speak to him at about 9:50 pm, he wasn't there. I went downstairs to the study and found my son-in-law in there. He was furious about something. I was just about to sit down when we heard Sofia's scream.'

MAX FISHER

- Internationally recognized movie star who went to school with Sofia and Linus
- Sociable, always fun at a party
- Has loved Sofia his entire life and has always been jealous of her husband

ALIBI

'I found Sofia crying on the stairs at around 9:45 pm. I gave her my jacket and we talked for about ten minutes. Then she went upstairs to redo her make-up and said she'd be back down in a minute. I was feeling hungry, so I went to the kitchen to get a snack and found Bletchley eating his dinner. That's when I heard that awful scream.'

➤ Go back to page 93.

LINUS BALDURSSON

- Magnus Baldursson's eldest child
- Quick-tempered and loud, but generally fun to be around
- Bankrupt after several bad business deals

ALIBI

'Yeah, I told my father about Sofia's debts – he deserved to know. Anyway, after the three of us argued, I went up to my room to think. I came down as soon as I heard the scream. That's when I found my sister's body.'

JAMES RUTHERFORD

- Has been married to Sofia for nine years
- Caring and dependable, but prone to fits of jealousy
- Frequently argues with his wife, but has never been violent

ALIBI

'I went to find my wife and saw her talking to Max on the stairs. It must have been just before 10:00 pm. He had his arm around her! I was so angry that I had to get away, so I went straight to the study to calm down! Magnus had just come in when we heard the scream.'

ALBERT BLETCHLEY

- Has served as the family butler for 36 years
- Hard-working, loyal and well-dressed
- Would do anything to protect the family

ALIBI

'Frankly, I'm glad Sofia's dead. She was always horrible to me and I never liked her. But it wasn't me who killed her. Ask Mr. Fisher. He was with me in the kitchen when it happened.'

6.2 Student A

A Complete the text with *a, an, the* or – (no article).

[1]___ Maasai of Kenya and Tanzania have several age traditions that lead into [2]___ manhood. Boys between [3]___ ages of 12 and 25 are taught to become [4]___ new warriors of [5]___ tribe. [6]___ night before [7]___ ceremony, they sleep outside in [8]___ forest, and at [9]___ sunrise they come back for singing and dancing. They drink [10]___ special drink, while also eating large amounts of [11]___ meat. For [12]___ next ten years they stay at [13]___ camp to learn to be warriors. After [14]___ final ceremony takes place, they become [15]___ senior warriors and can get married.

B You are going to explain the ceremony in Exercise A to your partner. Write notes to help you.

➤ Go back to page 67.

8.2 Student B

Use adjectives to describe the objects in the picture to your partner. Are there any similarities between your pictures?

There's a modern black camera in the bottom left-hand corner.

➤ Go back to page 91.

8.1 Student C

Read the story and write notes to help you summarize it for your group.

The Vanishing Hitchhiker

One night, a group of friends were driving to a dance when they spotted a young woman hitchhiking. The group decided to give the woman a ride and asked her to come to the party with them. She was obviously cold, so one of the group gave her a coat. They eventually got to the party and after a night of dancing, they drove the woman home. The next day, one of the friends remembered they had forgotten to ask for his coat back, so he drove to the woman's house. However, when he knocked on the door he was told by the couple that lived there that the woman had been killed in a car accident years before. Scared, the man drove back to the corner where he and his friends had met the woman the night before. There, hanging on a road sign, was his coat.

➤ Go back to page 89.

Communication Hub

8.1 Student A

Read the story and write notes to help you summarize it for your group.

TROJAN HORSE

The Trojan horse was a huge hollow wooden horse made by the Greeks during the Trojan War. The Greeks had pretended to give up in the war but had secretly sailed to the island of Tenedos. They had left one soldier, Sinon, to persuade the Trojans that the horse was an offering from the Greek gods. Laocoön and Cassandra, who were both important people in the city of Troy, warned against taking the horse into the city, but the Trojans accepted it anyway. In the middle of the night, Greek soldiers, who were hidden inside, emerged from the horse and let the rest of the Greek army into the city. The Greeks then captured and destroyed the city of Troy.

➤ Go back to page 89.

6.2 Student B

A Complete the text with *a, an, the* or – (no article).

The *fiesta de quince años* celebrates [1]___ girl's 15th birthday and is popular throughout [2]___ Latin America. In Argentina, Peru and some other countries, the girl traditionally arrives at the party with her father, wearing [3]___ elaborate dress. [4]___ pair then dance alone, before inviting [5]___ friends and family to join them. After this, the evening typically alternates between [6]___ three-course meal and more formal dances, before the father gives a speech and presents his daughter with [7]___ large cake. This stage of the evening usually involves [8]___ ritual in which female friends and family pull [9]___ ribbons from a bunch. Each of [10]___ ribbons has a lucky object attached to it, except for one which is attached to a ring. Whoever gets [11]___ ring is said to be the next person to get married.
In Cuba, the final dance involves dancing with 14 different people and blowing out [12]___ candle and collecting a rose after each dance. With each candle the girl gets [13]___ wish and then [14]___ flowers are given as [15]___ gift to her mother.

B You are going to explain the ceremony in Exercise A to your partner. Write notes to help you.

➤ Go back to page 67.

9.1 Student A

Read the situation below and role-play a conversation with your partner.

You have bought a new TV and it hasn't been working properly. Many of the functions don't work and other functions work really slowly. It's not the internet provider because your laptop and phone work fine. The product is still under warranty. You don't want it repaired because you have read online that these faults are common. You would like it replaced with a different model TV.

➤ Go back to page 101.

9.1 Quiz results

Are you a good complainer? *quiz results*

Mostly A's You don't like making a fuss, especially over things that just aren't very important. You'd rather put up with the mistake and get on with your day than get into an argument. You're also more than happy to face the consequences of your mistakes and wouldn't dream of blaming anyone else.

Mostly B's You're tired of big companies getting away with terrible customer service and see social media as the perfect place to fight for your rights. It's important to you that you get what you paid for and you're more than happy to publicly complain if you don't. After all, if you don't stand up to these companies, who will?

Mostly C's You don't see complaining as a way to get revenge. You understand that everyone makes mistakes, but expect a quick resolution when they affect you. You're more than willing to face the consequences of your own mistakes, but want to make sure steps are taken to help others avoid making the same mistakes in the future.

➤ Go back to page 100.

9.2 Groups

A Choose one of the products below to design an ad campaign around.

1. an electric sports car that is one of the most eco-friendly on the market
2. a sports brand directed toward wealthy young and successful people
3. a range of health-food products that are low in calories but nutritionally balanced
4. a fitness app that tracks all your activities and sets you new physical challenges

B Design an ad campaign around the product you chose in Exercise A. Use the following questions to help you:

1. How are you going to raise awareness of your product?
2. What high-profile celebrities would you get to endorse your product?
3. What trends are you going to link your product to?
4. What features will make customers fall in love with your product brand?
5. What is unique about your product compared to other products on the market?

➤ Go back to page 105.

8.1 Groups

Answer
It can't have been aliens since there were no signs of anything landing nearby. The family provided a sketch of one of the aliens which showed it must have been a large bird, probably a great horned owl. The sounds of bullets hitting metal must have been the surrounding farm buildings being hit.

➤ Go back to page 87.

8.1 Student B

Read the story and write notes to help you summarize it for your group.

The Loch Ness Monster

There are carvings from almost 1,500 years ago showing a huge monster in a Scottish lake and written reports from the 7th century describing the same creature. However, there were very few other reported sightings until 1933, when a doctor, Colonel Robert Wilson, took the famous photo of the supposed Loch Ness monster and sent it to a local newspaper in Inverness. They in turn then reported a sighting of an enormous creature in one of Scotland's largest lakes. However, in 1994, a man named Ian Wetherell confessed he had helped his father create the 'monster' using plastic and a toy submarine. His father had then given the photo to Wilson to submit to the papers because he thought people were more likely to believe a doctor. Despite the fact that people now know that the photo was a fake, there are still regular reports of sightings of the Loch Ness monster every year.

➤ Go back to page 89.

8.2 Student A

Use adjectives to describe the objects in the picture to your partner. Are there any similarities between your pictures?

There's a large old-fashioned camera in the top left-hand corner.

➤ Go back to page 91.

9.1 Student B

Read the situation below and role-play a conversation with your partner.

You have bought a new cell phone. It keeps turning off whenever you try to connect to wi-fi. The phone also crashes whenever you try to install a new operating system. The product is still under warranty. You don't want it repaired because you have read online that these faults are common. You would like it replaced with a different type of phone.

➤ Go back to page 101.

W — describing data

A Work in pairs. Which of these factors do you think are the most important things to consider when choosing a college or university? Why?

- quality of teaching
- college/university ranking
- friends at the college
- close to home
- good graduate employment rate
- cost of living

B Look at the bar chart. Which of the reasons in Exercise A is the most popular?

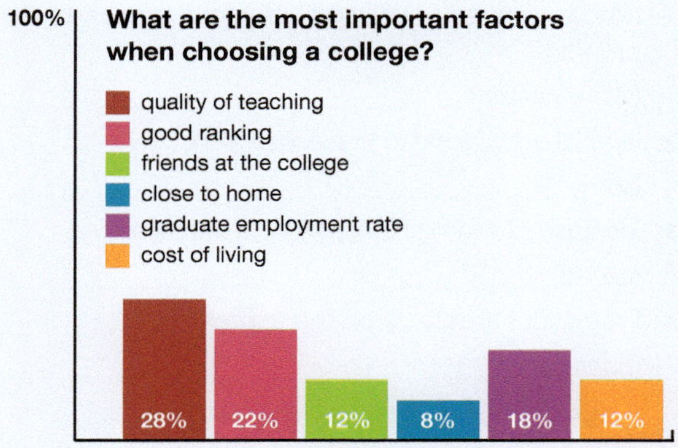

College choice

Introduction

The purpose of this report is to evaluate the results of a survey on reasons for choosing a college and to suggest areas for colleges to focus their efforts on to increase student recruitment.

Results

This graph illustrates the results of the student survey. The highest proportion of students chose the quality of teaching as the key factor. Almost one-third of students gave this as their primary reason for choosing which college or university to attend, with the institution's ranking being the second most import factor, according to almost a quarter of the students. The third most significant factor was employability of graduates, with friends and the cost of living more or less equal. The least important factor is closeness to home.

Interpretation

There are significant differences between two groups of factors in this data. Arguably, the first three factors are all interconnected. The ranking of a college can have an impact on employability and the standard of teaching has an impact on the ranking. Therefore, colleges need to focus not only on what is happening in the classroom, but also their connections with industry for internships and future employment. The other three factors are also potentially connected because they are clearly likely to have an impact on the students' lifestyle and happiness while attending college.

Recommendations

I would recommend that for colleges to increase their student recruitment and satisfaction they should invest in their staff and teaching facilities. They should also spend time developing their relationships with companies since employment opportunities are very important to students.

C Read the report and answer the questions.

1 How many sections are there to the report?

2 What is the difference between the results and interpretation sections?

3 What is the difference between the interpretation and recommendations sections?

D Complete the table with phrases from the report.

Describing data
Introduction
This report summarizes … and concludes with …
1 ________________
Evaluating results
The majority of …
2 ________________
The highest proportion of …
Several key trends indicated by the graph …
Comparing and contrasting
Similarly,
By contrast …
X and Y are 3 ________________
There is no difference between X and Y.
4 ________________ *X and Y.*
Making recommendations
It might also be useful to …
5 ________________

WRITING

A PREPARE You are going to write a report describing the data in the chart below and make recommendations to colleges about how to promote their course. Write notes on the key results and your recommendations.

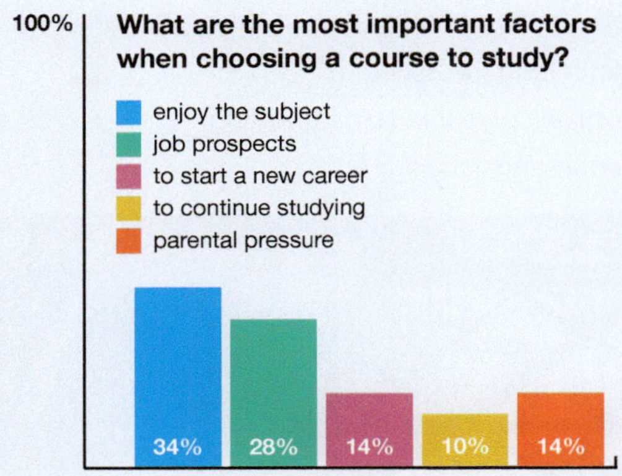

B PLAN Organize your notes into a report structure.

C WRITE Write your report. Use your plan to help you.

D EDIT Work in pairs. Edit your partner's report. Check:

- spelling and punctuation
- report structure
- strength of analysis and recommendations

Write a formal letter of complaint

W – hedging

A Work in pairs. Which of the following are issues in your neighborhood?

- graffiti
- trash
- crime
- noise pollution
- air pollution
- poor transportation systems
- lack of public spaces
- abandoned buildings

B Read the letter of complaint. What problem from Exercise A are mentioned?

Dear Sir/Madam,

[1]I am writing to you with regard to the proposal to knock down the old clothing factory and construct a new library in our area. While I agree that our neighborhood would benefit enormously from such a wonderful facility, I'm afraid I do not agree with the proposal for a number of reasons.

[2]First, the clothing factory is a historical building and something we should be looking to preserve and restore, not demolish. Instead of demolishing the factory, I feel that proposals should look at converting it into the library instead. Simply destroying such a landmark and starting again is not something I expect many residents will find acceptable. Second, the current suggestion will create unacceptable levels of noise and take significantly longer than converting the factory. This is not something I feel residents will put up with and I have no option but to organize a campaign group against this.

[3]I feel that local residents should be consulted on this project and I would appreciate an open discussion on these plans. I look forward to hearing from you on this matter.

Kind regards,

John Hadland

C Match the paragraphs (1–3) to their function (a–c).

a describing the issues ___

b explaining your reason for writing ___

c requesting action ___

D Rewrite the sentences using the words in parentheses. Use the information in the box and the letter to help you.

Hedging

Hedges are used to soften an opinion, rather than simply saying 'I don't agree.' Instead of directly disagreeing, which might be seen as being rude, people usually write something such as *I'm sorry but I don't agree.* Hedging like this makes your opinion or suggestion less direct and less likely to cause offense.

1 I know we need a new road but I don't agree with the proposal.
(*While / afraid*) ______________________.

2 It is not acceptable to lose a local park.
(*sorry*) ______________________.

3 Most people won't be happy with the plan.
(*expect*) ______________________.

4 I want your assistance on this matter.
(*appreciate*) ______________________.

WRITING

A PREPARE You are going to write a letter of complaint about a proposal to build a new road through your local park. Write notes about potential issues with this proposal and possible alternatives.

B PLAN Organize your notes into a formal letter structure.

C WRITE Write your letter of complaint. Use your plan to help you.

D EDIT Work in pairs. Edit your partner's letter. Check:

- spelling and punctuation
- strength of analysis and recommendations
- use of hedging language

W– writing conclusions

A Read the essay prompt and answer the questions.

1 What claim is made in the prompt?

2 What does *this* refer to in the first question?

Many former criminals go on to reoffend following their release from prison. Is the prison system primarily to blame for this? Should more be done to support former criminals?

B Read the introduction and body of the essay. Choose the best summary (1 or 2) of the writer's position.

1 Support groups need to be established in local areas to help former criminals establish valuable roles in society.

2 The prison system needs to do more to provide criminals with the skills they need to succeed post release.

A large proportion of former criminals go on to reoffend when released from prison. This essay will explain that while the prison system certainly plays a role in this statistic, it is primarily the lack of employment opportunities on the outside that is to blame and, for this reason, support networks must be established to better integrate ex-convicts back into society.

One of the primary functions of the prison system is to reform criminals, not just punish them. To this end, most prisons offer training programs that provide inmates that are willing to learn with practical skills that should help them find employment post-release. However, many former criminals return to neighborhoods where opportunities are limited and they are forced to take low-paid jobs that don't reflect the skills they acquired while behind bars. Without a clear support network designed to help shape the careers of former criminals, many feel neglected by society. It is this lack of support that is the root of reoffending.

While most governments do offer guidance to former criminals, much more needs to be done to support sustainable reintegration into society. Support groups formed primarily of ex-convicts that have forged successful careers post-release should be founded in all major towns and cities. These groups should be given all of the funding and resources necessary to nurture the careers of former criminals, ensuring that they can play a valuable part in society.

C Work in pairs. Which is the best conclusion for the essay in Exercise B? Use the information in the box to help you.

Writing conclusions

Essays should finish with a simple conclusion summarizing the key arguments made in the body. Since no new ideas should be explored in the conclusion, it's easy to lose the interest of readers at this point. To avoid this, ensure your conclusions are short, simple and paraphrase your main ideas.

1

In conclusion, while most prisons offer training programs that provide inmates with valuable practical skills, many ex-convicts return to neighborhoods where opportunities are limited. All too frequently, they find themselves surrounded by others who have returned to a life of crime and cannot resist the urge to follow suit. By establishing support groups in major towns and cities, we would ensure that former criminals play a valuable part in society instead of turning back to a life of crime.

2

In conclusion, although the prison system should certainly shoulder some of the blame for the high volume of repeat offenders, it does provide inmates with the opportunity to acquire practical skills that are valuable to society. However, the existing networks available post-release do not offer former criminals the level of support they need in order to apply what they have learned. We need to establish well-resourced support networks throughout the country to help ex-convicts forge successful careers.

WRITING

A PREPARE Read the essay question below and brainstorm ideas.

Many ex-convicts struggle to adapt to life outside prison post-release. Is their attitude primarily to blame for this? Should more be done to help them adjust?

B PLAN Organize your ideas into paragraphs.

C WRITE Write your essay. Use your plan to help you.

D EDIT Work in pairs. Edit your partner's essay. Check:

- spelling and punctuation
- use of language
- strength of conclusion

W— using discourse markers in formal writing

A Read the proposal task below and answer the questions that follow.

> Your hotel has been getting low ratings from users on a popular travel website. Your boss has asked you to look at the reviews and to write a proposal for changes that can be made to the hotel. You should include information about the weaknesses reviewers have mentioned and suggest improvements.

1 What is the current problem?
2 What recommendations do you need to make?

Proposal for improvements to the hotel

Introduction

The purpose of this proposal is to examine weaknesses identified in the hotel's online reviews and to suggest ways to address them.

Hotel weaknesses

Analysis of the reviews has revealed that most customers feel the hotel décor is dated and in much need of modernization. In fact, many feel the old-fashioned look of the hotel makes it feel unclean. Furthermore, consumers usually leave poor reviews of the food in the hotel restaurant. The menu is considered to be too limited, and the service during breakfast too slow. Consequently, fewer and fewer guests are eating in the hotel itself.

Hotel improvements

Modernizing the look of the hotel would be hugely beneficial since there seems to be little doubt that we are attracting fewer customers as a result of the outdated décor. The hotel should be given a simple, fresh and clean look that is more in keeping with our competitors. The restaurant should be a way for the hotel to maximize profits, but due to the limited menu and poor service, people are choosing to eat elsewhere. Therefore, updating the menu and hiring more service staff is essential.

Recommendations

Implementation of the ideas outlined above would result in an increased level of customer satisfaction and more positive online reviews. Improving the restaurant would also encourage more guests to dine in, increasing overall profitability.

B Read the proposal. According to the writer, what are the main weaknesses of the hotel? What solutions do they recommend?

C Underline four formal discourse markers in the text. Use the information in the box to help you.

Using discourse markers in formal writing

In formal writing, we use a range of discourse markers to connect ideas. These include adding ideas (e.g. *additionally*), talking about effects and results (e.g. *subsequently*) and giving examples (e.g. *for instance*).

D Complete the sentences using discourse markers from Exercise C.

1 The hotel has had little investment in recent years. ________________, the volume of reservations has fallen.
2 ________________ the limited menu, customers are leaving negative reviews online.
3 A lot of our customers said they received poor service. ________________, many complained our staff was rude.
4 The new menu simply isn't popular. ________________, we should reinstate the old one.

WRITING

A PREPARE Work in pairs. Read the proposal task below. Brainstorm issues a coffee chain might experience and how to address them.

> You work for a large, successful coffee chain. However, lately your customer service department has been receiving increasingly negative reviews on social media. You have been asked to write a proposal highlighting the main issues and how to address them.

B PLAN Organize your ideas into appropriate sections.

C WRITE Write your proposal. Use your plan to help you.

D EDIT Work in pairs. Edit your partner's proposal. Check:

- spelling and punctuation
- strength of analysis and recommendations
- use of formal discourse markers

W — concession

A Read the essay question below and answer the questions that follow.

Some think social media has a negative impact on individuals and society as a whole. Others argue the effects have largely been positive. Discuss both views and give your opinion.

1 What two points of view do you need to discuss?

2 What else do you need to do?

B Work in pairs. What positive and negative effects do you think the writer might discuss?

C Read the essay. Were any of your ideas from Exercise B mentioned?

Social media has had a huge impact on people's lives, and in recent years, many have argued that this effect has been detrimental to both individuals and society as a whole. Although there are undeniably many negative effects of social media, I believe that its impact on society has been predominantly beneficial.

It must be acknowledged that social media brings with it a number of negative consequences. Arguably, as we spend more and more of our time online, we're engaging far less in the real world. As a result, as much as some people may feel they have a great deal of support from their online community, they are potentially losing touch with valuable support networks around them. Furthermore, because of the anonymous nature of online communities, interaction is frequently very confrontational, or worse – guided by people whose only agenda seems to be to cause conflict or to promote controversial views.

Nevertheless, despite these potential issues, the advantages of social media are apparent in many aspects of our lives. First, it has enabled people to stay in touch with a wider group of friends, which they might otherwise have lost contact with. Additionally, these platforms provide a simple way to connect and share content with people around the world that have common interests – something that, while possible before social media, was certainly far more difficult.

Overall, although social media can lead to conflict and the breakdown of face-to-face communication with those around us, it has also made many bonds stronger.

D Scan the essay again. Underline the words and phrases used to make concessions. Use the information in the box to help you.

Concession

In writing, concession means admitting that part or all of an opposing viewpoint is valid. Doing so not only shows you have a well-rounded view of the topic, but can also be used to further develop your own argument.

***While** it's true that social media can make some people feel isolated, the majority of us feel better connected in this day and age.*

E Rewrite the sentences using the words in bold.

1 Social media allows for more open discussion. It frequently leads to conflict.
While … may
_______________.

2 Social media divides some people. It brings many more together.
Although … may
_______________.

3 It's clear that many people enjoy using social media. It makes others feel isolated.
Many … but
_______________.

4 I don't like the idea of policing social media. It's an important next step.
Nevertheless
_______________.

5 I don't like social media personally. I can understand its appeal.
As much as
_______________.

WRITING

A PREPARE Read the essay question below and brainstorm your ideas.

Today, many people prefer to socialize online rather than in person. Some people feel this is a positive development while others argue it has had a negative impact on our relationships. Discuss both views and give your opinion.

B PLAN Organize your notes from Exercise A into an appropriate essay structure.

C WRITE Write your essay. Use your plan to help you.

D EDIT Work in pairs. Edit your partner's essay. Check:

- spelling and punctuation
- strength of arguments
- use of concession phrases

UNIT 6

Lesson 6.1 Listening, Exercise B

6.1 **P = Presenter J = Jessica A = Andrew**

P: Hello, and welcome to another edition of *Society Today*. I'm your host Rachel Baxter. So the global school rankings are out again, and they seem to indicate that stricter schooling systems get better results. Here to discuss whether it's time we moved toward a stricter schooling system in the US are Andrew Jones, head of the Lighthouse Academy in Michigan, a school well-known for its 'no nonsense' approach, and mother-of-two, Jessica Wilding. Jessica recently removed her children from a school in Grand Rapids, Michigan because as she thought the rules there were simply too strict. Good morning, both of you.

J and A: Good morning.

P: So Jessica, you went to a very open and relaxed school where children were allowed to pretty much do whatever they wanted.

J: Uh, yes, that's right. We weren't forced to do anything we didn't want to. Teachers and students were treated as equals. Every semester a vote was held so we could decide on rules together. I loved this system and was disappointed to find my children didn't have this level of freedom.

P: So you put them in another school?

J: I did, and I think it was the right decision. The school they're at now is great. Amazing, in fact. The only rule they have is that their actions must not harm anyone else. Every week they have a school meeting and vote on all sorts of issues together. I thrived under this kind of system and I think my children will, too.

A: I'm sorry, but it sounds ridiculous to me. Students that get to decide their own rules will use it as an excuse to behave badly.

J: I'm sorry, but that simply isn't true. Students don't need to follow old-fashioned rules to understand what they should or shouldn't do. Students behave well when they are given power to decide what they can't do. I think this is really important, especially for teenagers.

A: Well, I couldn't work in such a system! Rules are important.

J: I completely agree, but I think students should have a say in exactly what those rules are. I genuinely feel that most problems with teenagers come because we make them follow rules, but they're growing into adults and simply want more control of their environment. They can make very sensible decisions when given trust.

P: But surely students given this much freedom will just choose not to go to classes?

A: Exactly!

J: I'm not sure. In my school, students weren't obliged to attend classes. We could also move up a year group earlier than normal or stay back a little longer if we felt like we needed more time. We could choose our subjects and didn't have to take ones we didn't like. We could even repeat things if we wanted. People weren't left behind.

A: That's very interesting actually. How did they decide when you took exams?

J: Well, in many cases people took subjects and exams earlier than they were supposed to. If you enjoy a subject, you want to do well in it. I don't think students should be required to go to classes or to study certain subjects. If you struggle in physics and you're not ever really going to use it in the future, why study it?

A: Now that I can't agree with. People end up …

J: Why on earth not? The exam results in our school were excellent. Many students managed to get into excellent colleges and go on to have very good careers.

A: Yes, but people end up working in all sorts of jobs they never thought they would have. If you don't get a well-rounded education, it could massively affect your future.

P: Interesting! Now Andrew, you're head of one of the strictest schools in the US, and you also had a similar experience as a child yourself. Why do you think it works?

A: I believe that young students need structure. They simply need to know what the rules are.

P: Could you give us some examples of the types of strict rules you had as a child?

A: Sure. We weren't allowed to have dirty shoes. Basically, everyone had to look the same – no unusual haircuts, the same bag, the same hairbands and even the same coats. We weren't allowed to talk to each other or look at the clock. We also had to focus on our work and we weren't allowed to misbehave and distract others.

J: Not distracting people and talking – fine. But does it really matter what color your hair is or what bag you have? That seems ridiculous.

A: I've put many of the same rules in place in my school.

P: What happened if you broke the rules?

A: We had to wear a tag around our neck with a message such as 'I have 24 hours to straighten up my uniform' if we looked sloppy. If we behaved badly in class, we had to study on our own. We were forced to do this for five classes. Hundreds of children had to do this. I have similar rules in my school.

J: You're joking! How embarrassing!

A: The students are better behaved.

J: Oh, come on! I don't think the punishment fits the crime there. I agree children are supposed to learn right from wrong but being forced to study on their own for wearing the wrong color hairband! That's clearly unreasonable. The punishment should fit the crime.

P: That seems sensible to me. So, Andrew did you enjoy your experience at school?

A: I did. You quickly learned what you needed to do. You got to know what the rules were and how you were expected to behave. It actually made it really fair having more rules. We didn't have the 'strict' teacher because they were all strict. I was really happy there. We had a lot of fun. We went on some amazing school trips. We had all the usual sports teams and parties. It was great!

J: Just don't break the rules! I suppose I just loved my school. I felt like an equal and included. I think it actually made me more mature when I went to college. A lot of people see that moment as 'freedom', but we had had that for years. That time at school was the happiest time of my life, actually.

A: Me too!

P: Interesting that such different systems made you both happy. Thank you for coming in today.

J: Thanks for inviting us!

A: Great to be here.

P: Next on the show, we have several students from …

Lesson 6.1 Reading, Exercise A

6.5 **P = Presenter J = Jane**

P: Welcome back. Joining me now to talk about her new movie is the actress Jane Nash. So Jane, you've just finished work on your latest movie, an adaptation of the book *Agnes Grey*. When is the book set?

J: It's set at the beginning of the 19th century, when very few people in England went to school. Children generally had to work to earn money for their family. Only rich families could afford to send their children to school. I mean there were some scholarships for boys from poor backgrounds, but not for girls.

P: Shocking to think that so recently not everyone got an education!

J: I know. And it's not like it was easy to get a scholarship. Only the brightest could pass the entrance exam. If a family was rich, a girl might attend a boarding school but more likely she had a governess who taught her at home.

P: A governess? Sounds like a pretty serious person! And that's who you play, isn't it?

J: Yes, I play Agnes Grey, a governess. A governess was usually a well-educated woman who needed to earn money to support her family. They were pretty much a well-educated babysitter, though.

P: Doesn't sound like a fun job.

J: No, it was tough. You could have some terribly behaved children and no support or help. Life could be terrible for a governess! It was supposed to be homeschooling but it was part parenting, part discipline and a tiny bit of education.

P: Interesting! OK, so now we have a short clip from the movie to show people …

Lesson 6.2 Listening, Exercise E

6.8 **I = Interviewer J = Janice Ka = Kayley R = Robbie**

1

I: So Janice, you started your own business when you were 70.

J: Yes, it all started soon after I had grandchildren. They're amazing, but exhausting! I live around the corner from my daughter and so I used to do her a favor and take care of the grandchildren a couple of mornings a week. Every time they came over, I would, uh, make up games or do activities and that kind of thing, you know. They absolutely loved doing arts and crafts! Well, to be honest, I enjoyed it as well. If I tried to do anything else, they were just really hard to control. They weren't doing any harm, they were just full of energy – running around and shouting constantly. It was just noise! But with arts and crafts, they would sit there and focus on what they were doing. Taking care of the kids turned out to be a blessing in disguise because it led to me starting my business.

I: How did that happen?

J: Well, I'd kind of always wanted my own business, but never been brave enough. One year, I organized my granddaughter's birthday party around arts and crafts and they all loved it. I was worried about setting up my own business, but I decided to bite the bullet and set up a pottery café in my seventies. The parents love it. They can get involved with the kids or just sit and have a cup of coffee.

I: And how well has the business done?

J: Well, you know, it's hard, but I'm doing my best. Like any business, really, we had a loss in the first year. Now we're making a profit. I'm not rolling in money but I make enough. But really I'm so happy I've made a success out of this. It's the first job I've ever loved! I wish I'd done it sooner.

2

I: Hi Kayley, how old are you?

Ka: I'm fourteen.

I: And you're about to start college?

Ka: Yeah, I know. Weird or what? I'm off to study English Literature in September. I took my school exams four years early and achieved A grades in all of them.

I: That's amazing! Why do you think you are so successful academically?

Ka: I don't know. I think, well, I think most people could do the same if they got their act together. I didn't find school that difficult to be honest. It's not exactly rocket science, is it? Anyway, age is just a number. I think schools should do away with age restrictions for taking exams. Some people are ready much earlier than others.

I: Are you worried about going to college at such a young age? Most people go when they are 18 or 19.

Ka: Definitely! What are the other kids gonna make of me? It's going to be difficult to have a good social life, but that only makes up a small part of the college experience. People are generally nice, and I think they'll make allowances for my age. I hope I make a good impression, but I am a little worried.

I: And what do you hope to do when you graduate?

Ka: I love making up my own stories and really hope to be a children's book author. I write and illustrate stories for my younger cousins and they love them.

3

I: So Robbie, you've always had a terrible fear of heights and flying. You were 28 when you first went on a plane. So, how did you get over your fear?

R: Well, I was getting married about five years ago and my wife really wanted to go to the Maldives for our honeymoon, but she knew that wasn't an option. She cut me a lot of slack and didn't push for a trip because she knew I was terrified! She did start looking for vacation spots in the US, but I could tell she wasn't happy. She was trying to make the best of the situation by doing without the exciting honeymoon, but I felt so guilty. I decided to try hypnotherapy to see if that would get rid of my fear. Amazingly, it worked!

I: But since then you have really embraced not being afraid of heights and flying, right?

R: Yes, I've taken up flying and I'm now a certified pilot. I've done ten parachute jumps from a plane as well, and tried bungee jumping and base jumping.

I: That's amazing. A whole new world opened up to you!

R: Totally! My wife now gets slightly annoyed with how much time I spend doing these things, but we do have a lot more fun and exciting vacations!

UNIT 7

Lesson 7.1 Listening, Exercise B

7.1 **P = Presenter**

P: I grew up in a poor, inner-city neighborhood in Greater Manchester in the UK. This is what my neighborhood looked like when I was a kid – abandoned factories, empty blocks of apartments and playgrounds covered in broken glass and graffiti. I couldn't wait to leave, so I worked hard and got into King's College in London. Life in the south was great, but I couldn't stop thinking about my hometown and what it could have been. So, when I graduated, I moved back to Manchester and started the Open Spaces project. The goal of the project was simple – find buildings and spaces that have been abandoned and turn them into something that would better serve the community.

Our first project was an old industrial estate by the river. It hadn't been used for years and nature had naturally taken over. There was a plan to knock down the old buildings and construct new offices, but we thought it would be better as a space for the local community. We had to fight against developers to keep the land. So, how did we manage to get the local council to give us the land? Well, we approached it from an educational perspective. Many kids in large cities like this never have any experience of the countryside or wildlife, so we campaigned to develop an education center for schools across the city. Now, we have an area of local plants and wildlife for children to explore. We've also built a space for teaching the children about the local wildlife and the importance of protecting the environment in general. There are also bike paths for local people to use. So, was it a success? Absolutely. In fact, if we maintain our current numbers, we will have had 15,000 visitors in our first year. For many of the kids this is their only experience of having been shown nature.

The council was so inspired by the success of the community park that they asked us to look for similar opportunities around the city. When we found this old warehouse north of the river, we decided to turn it into a gallery. We wanted to use it to inspire young people to get into art. We got local artists to produce original pieces for the opening and to contribute any other work they had that reflected the city. We have both indoor and outdoor spaces for people to exhibit their work. To involve the local community more, we also have a section dedicated to art produced by local school children. For two weeks every year a different school gets to exhibit their students' work. The children are so inspired by this. Their work is alongside real artists' work. They come down with their families and friends and they're amazed to see their work on display. If we give kids opportunities like this, what are they going to achieve in the future? That's what I find really inspiring!

So, by this point we'd created a community park and a public art gallery. So what next? Well, in a lot of poor areas there are really high levels of obesity. Families eat takeout and microwave meals. They don't eat fresh produce because they find that it's too expensive. So, when we found a small space of wasteland that wasn't used and was largely full of garbage, we decided to build a large community garden. People are free to take the produce we grow in the garden. They can leave a donation if they want but they don't have to. We built an organic café by the entrance and use the profit to maintain the garden. Everyone who works there is a volunteer. Any leftover food from the café is given away at the end of the day to homeless people. This has been by far the most inspiring project. People are starting to use public land all across the city to start small food gardens. Now, there are nearly 20 such gardens across the city. If you're thinking about starting a garden, speak to me later. A few years ago I'd never grown anything; now I'm somewhat of an expert – especially in zucchini!

If we don't come together as a community, neighborhoods like mine will fall apart. We need people to help us take this forward. To take back our city and transform people's lives. Whether you want to start a skate park, an outdoor music venue or simply another organic garden. If you care about your community, do something to improve it. People like you can help bring back the community spirit we've lost. All it takes is a good idea and a little hard work. Thank you.

Lesson 7.2 Listening, Exercise C
7.5 **I = Interviewer C = Callum**

I: Joining us next is activist and founder of the Free Life Project, Callum Castling. Callum, welcome to the show.

C: Thanks for inviting me.

I: So Callum, for some years now, you've been involved in a movement to set up a moneyless society.

C: That's correct.

I: So, how did you get started? What inspired you?

C: Well, obviously I look up to people like Mark Boyle. He's achieved amazing things. But it sort of all started in my son's bedroom.

I: Really?

C: Yeah, so my wife was pregnant with our first son and I needed to redecorate our spare bedroom. The thing is, I'm an accountant. I'm great with numbers, but not so good with anything practical. Anyway, luckily, I get along really well with my neighbors and one of them is a professional decorator. Anyway, it turned out he was looking for an accountant, so we came up with a plan to help us both. I started to do his accounts and he did some painting and decorating around the house. We've been friends ever since.

I: So, is that what inspired your Facebook group?

C: Yeah, that's right. I just thought there must be a lot of people in the community that could help each other out. So, I set up the Facebook group to give people somewhere to share their skills or give away things they don't want anymore. It actually helps cut down on waste as well.

I: Right, so what kind of things do people get rid of?

C: Anything, really. Old bikes ... couches ... one guy even gave away his ex-girlfriend's stuff she had left at his house!

I: Really? So, has the group been popular?

C: Well, yes and no. We only have about a thousand followers, but they are all pretty active.

I: So, why did you decide to move things offline?

C: Well, social media is great, but it can feel pretty impersonal at times. We had a lot of great ideas that we'd never get around to working on because we rarely met. Basically, we felt like a community with no home. So we scouted around the city, looking for a space to use and found an old abandoned factory. It was great but needed a lot of work.

I: How did you get the money to renovate it?

C: Well, the factory was owned by the council and once we explained what we were trying to do, they offered to let us use it until they were able to sell the land. Then we managed to renovate it for free.

I: For free?

C: Yep. We got all of the materials via our Facebook group. People volunteered their time and skills. It was amazingly easy really to get a lot of volunteer workers. We got building materials, plants, gardening equipment. We even managed to get all of our tables and chairs and kitchen equipment from a local restaurant that was closing down. I couldn't believe it. People were just so generous.

I: And what do you do with the space?

C: It's become our community center, really. Twice a week we have a general networking event. We provide drinks and snacks and anyone who is interested in sharing their skills or needs to find someone with a particular skill can come along. It's great because if you come up against a problem then you can usually find someone here to help. People have started car-sharing systems, food banks to help the poor – all sorts of things really. Or you can just start something you're interested in – a language exchange, clubs, societies. You name it, people are starting it!

I: Sounds amazing!

C: People love it. Let's face it, it's more comfortable meeting someone face-to-face than just talking briefly on the phone or on a website. If something is really popular, many people are happy to run a workshop to teach people. This can be anything from basic bike maintenance to teaching people to find food in the countryside.

I: What else have you done?

C: We used the free kitchen equipment to set up a local café. And we've used the outdoor space for a kitchen garden, so everything in the café comes from local farms or our own garden.

I: I must come for lunch sometime!

C: You should! The food is actually pretty good.

I: So, do you do any other interesting things?

C: One thing we always organize is regular parties. People like to come together to socialize with the people near them. We have two or three big street parties every year. You know, like a barbecue using the produce from the garden.

I: Well, it sounds like you're restoring a good old-fashioned sense of community.

C: I think we are. People move around so much these days, they rarely get to know their neighbors. Groups like ours bring people together and show them what can be achieved when they start to help each other out.

I: Thank you for coming in today, Callum. Hopefully, some of our listeners will take inspiration from your group and start their own community projects.

UNIT 8

Lesson 8.1 Listening, Exercise B
8.1 **I = Interviewer P = Phillip**

I: Hello, and welcome to *Connections*. On this week's show, we're talking about the influence storytelling has on our culture. Why do so many countries have different variations of the same story? How do these stories grow and change? Here to help us answer these questions is Philip Norris, author of *The Myths That Made Us*, a new book about the history of storytelling. Phillip, welcome to the show.

P: Good morning. Thank you for inviting me.

I: Great that you can be here. Now, I'd always imagined that myths and legends were very specific to each culture. I thought they were essentially the mythical stories that people listened to before books. Is that not the case?

P: Well, in some ways it is. You're right that each culture has its own myths and legends that are specific to them, but what we do have is common themes across all of them. These myths appear across places and societies that are thousands of miles apart, at a time when there would have been very little contact between these groups, so they can't have the same origins. However, there are striking similarities between these stories.

I: One story we all hear about in England when we are growing up is the legend of King Arthur and the Knights of the Round Table. A king of Britain who defended the country and led a group of knights against invaders. It's almost certainly not true and there are a lot of different versions with tales of his heroic deeds. Do other countries have such myths?

P: Very much so. This is something I would refer to as a 'Hero Myth'. I think this is common across all cultures. Some of the oldest books in many countries are essentially heroic tales – an individual fighting their way across lands on a mission to save someone or find something.

I: Do you have a particular favorite hero myth?

P: Yes. I love the tales of Sinbad the Sailor and his adventures at sea. In the original stories, Sinbad goes on seven voyages across the seas off East Africa and South Asia where he finds whales the size of islands, giant snakes and rivers filled with diamonds.

I: So, can you tell us a little more about one of the stories?

P: Of course. So the third voyage of Sinbad is probably one of the most exciting. As in many of the stories, Sinbad's ship is caught in a terrible storm and driven off course. They sail toward a small island but are attacked by a tribe of monkeys carrying spears. Fearing for their lives, Sinbad and his crew swim to the island and rush to a castle they see at the top of a hill. Tired and hungry from their escape, the crew falls asleep on the floor of the castle but are awoken to find the ground shaking. In the doorway to their room, stands a giant over 20 meters tall. His eyes burn like fire, his teeth are long and sharp, and his huge mouth has the lips of a camel. Sinbad and his crew try to run away, but one of them is caught and eaten by the giant.

I: Wow! So how does Sinbad escape?

P: Well, you'll just have to read the story for yourself. I don't want to spoil the ending!

I: Fair enough. So it seems that dragons and other strange creatures appear across many cultures. Why do you think that is?

P: Well, I think many of them were inspired by people finding the fossils of ancient creatures. Some are pure fantasy, though. Take the Greek myth of Medusa, who was a winged human with poisonous snakes in her hair. In the myth, anyone who looks at her face turns to stone. King Polydectes decides to send Perseus to kill Medusa. The hero Perseus is able to kill her by looking into a mirrored shield and chopping off her head. This myth also connects to other cultures as well though, such as the Berbers in Morocco. However, monster myths are not only present in ancient legends; we have many that still exist today. One that exists in many cultures is a variation of a giant human-like creature such as the Yeti in the Himalayas or Bigfoot in North America. Even today, we still create new stories that have striking similarities across cultures. We usually refer to these as urban myths or urban legends.

I: So are urban legends just modern tales about mythical creatures?

P: Many of them do involve monsters, but others focus on ghosts or murderers. One of the most popular stories in modern culture is of a person appearing in a mirror or bathroom. In Japan, this is known as Hanako-San, when the spirit of a young girl appears in school bathrooms. People have to knock three times on the third stall door and ask, 'Are you there Hanako-San?'. A small girl or a white hand appears from the stall. This is very similar to the Bloody Mary myth in America and many others around the world. It's largely a game for young children, for whom the stories are very believable, to test their bravery, and it's surprisingly similar across the world. As are various other tales about ghosts, murders and other strange events. I guess it just shows the way our ancestors interpreted the world around them differently.

I: Thank you for coming in today, this has been really interesting. For those of you interested in finding out more, Philip's book, *The Myths That Made Us*, is out this Friday.

8.4 Lesson 8.2 Listening, Exercise B
L = Lecturer

L: So, I want you all to think of an event from your childhood. Something that makes you smile every time you remember it. Got it? OK, now try to picture that event in your mind. Think about where you were, who you were with, what you could hear, what you could smell … most importantly, think about how you felt. I bet you can remember everything pretty clearly, right? Well, I don't want to upset anyone, but when it comes to accurately recalling events, the human memory is pretty awful. We like to think that our memories are like recordings we can access and watch whenever we want. Yet in reality, our memories change over time. Each time we recall an event, we rewrite the memory – adding details, updating things to match our current knowledge. Sometimes we combine two memories into one. Sometimes we even create memories. Sounds far-fetched, doesn't it? But actually, in study after study, a surprisingly high proportion of people have described memories of events that they cannot possibly have personally experienced.

'False memory syndrome' – the creation of entirely false memories – first came to the attention of the public in the late 1980s. At the time, many therapists believed that people who had experienced something terrible in their lives blocked out the memory of it, locking it deep in their minds and that the only way to access these 'repressed memories' was through therapy. Belief in this idea spread quickly, and many people who had gone into therapy looking for help with anxiety or depression were horrified to be told that they had blocked out the memory of a terrible experience years before. However, during the 90s, the theory was heavily criticized and, in the years since, multiple studies have strongly suggested that the therapists were actually encouraging their patients to create false memories. But how is this possible? How can we encourage someone to remember something that never actually happened? To help us answer this, we need to look back at the work of the American cognitive psychologist, Elizabeth Loftus.

Loftus actually first started exploring the idea of false memories in the 1970s. She did this by showing people simulations of crimes and accidents, then asking them what they remembered. In a landmark study in 1974, Loftus showed a video of a simulated car crash and asked one group, 'How fast were the cars traveling when they hit each other?' She asked another group, 'How fast were the cars traveling when they smashed into each other?' Interestingly, when asked the question with the more dramatic verb, *smashed*, witnesses said the car was traveling faster. They were also more likely to say they saw broken glass flying through the air, even though this didn't actually happen. In other studies, researchers changed some of the details when discussing an accident and many of the participants added this information to their memory – they essentially rewrote what they remembered happening, simply because they were encouraged to by the interviewer.

So, why is this important? Well, studies like this clearly demonstrate that the way you ask questions or discuss an event can strongly influence someone's memory of it. Loftus and many others like her suspected that this went some way in explaining why so many people in the 1980s were suddenly remembering horrifying experiences from their childhood. The therapists, whether intentionally or not, might actually have been encouraging patients to rewrite their own memories. But could people have been encouraged to create entirely new memories?

In 1995, Loftus designed an experiment to test this very idea. In the study, participants were given a booklet containing four short stories about themselves, three of which were true and one which never actually happened. The false story described how when they were younger, they'd gotten lost in a shopping mall, cried and were eventually helped by an elderly woman. During the study, participants were asked to write down as much detail as they could remember about each of the four stories. One in three remembered getting lost in the shopping mall, despite the fact that this never actually happened. In the 23 years since the shopping mall experiment, multiple studies have supported the idea that, under the right conditions, it is possible to encourage people to create entirely false memories.

If this is true, then I'd argue that we need to seriously reconsider the use of eyewitness testimony in the courtroom. The information presented by a witness may have been influenced by the way in which they were questioned after the event. On top of that, lawyers could encourage witnesses to add or change details. Think about how many innocent people might have been wrongfully convicted of a crime they didn't commit on the strength of an entirely false memory.

To most of us, our memories form the basis of our identity. They represent who we are and where we came from. But the research of Loftus and others like her shows that we cannot reliably distinguish between real and false memories, and in the courtroom, this could change the lives of innocent people forever. Thank you.

UNIT 9

Lesson 9.1 Listening, Exercise C

9.3 **R = Recorded message A = Amy C = Customer**

R: Thank you for holding, we appreciate your call. A customer service operator will be with you in approximately two minutes.

A: Good morning, Top Books, Amy speaking. Sorry to keep you waiting.

C: Finally! I've been on hold for 40 minutes! Aren't you supposed to answer within five minutes?

A: That is our goal sir, yes, but we've been experiencing an unusually high number of calls today. Again, I apologize for the delay, sir. How can I help you today?

C: I'm calling to complain about the condition of the books I received.

A: Oh, I'm sorry to hear that. What seems to be the problem?

C: Well, whoever delivered them left the box out in our backyard. We were away that weekend and it was raining pretty heavily so some of the books got damaged.

A: I see. OK. Could I just take your name and order number?

C: Of course. It's Harry Jenkins and the order number is 077-ADEP-9261.

A: Thank you. OK, here we are. Right, so it says here that the books were delivered on the 12th, and that your safe place is the backyard. Is that right?

C: Well … yes, but it obviously isn't safe from the rain!

A: I appreciate that, sir, although according to our terms of service, all deliveries are left in a safe place specified by the customer.

C: I understand that, but at no point did I consent to the books being left somewhere they could get damaged! It shows a complete lack of common sense. Underneath the patio table, that's where they should have been left. Or even in the children's playhouse. At least then they would have been protected from the elements! I'm sorry, but it simply isn't good enough. It's just terrible customer service!

A: I'm very sorry you feel that way, sir. How would you like us to address the issue?

C: A full refund, that's what I expect.

A: Well, while I am sympathetic to your situation, the books were delivered in accordance with our terms of service.

C: I understand that, but I really must insist on a full refund.

A: I'm afraid that since we have adhered to your delivery instructions, the most I'd be able to offer is $10 off your next purchase.

C: Are you joking? Those books cost me $150! More to the point, why would I want to buy anything from you again when my first purchase has been such a disaster? If you can't offer a refund, I'd like all of the books picked up and replaced.

A: I see … And, are all of the books damaged?

C: To a certain extent, yes, although some are much worse than others.

A: Well, maybe we could explore some other options? How about replacing the most damaged books?

C: Absolutely not! Why should I have to pay for damaged books? If your delivery driver had used a little common sense, we wouldn't be in this situation in the first place.

A: Well, as I mentioned earlier, we have followed …

C: Look, I don't want to argue about this anymore! If you don't replace all of the books, I'll take my complaint higher. And I'll be posting about the poor service on social media; I can assure you of that!

A: I'm sure that won't be necessary, sir. I'll register your complaint in our system and someone will be in touch within 24 hours to discuss what happens next.

C: 24 hours? Why can't this be dealt with right now? What is the point of speaking to you if you can't help me?

A: I can only apologize for any inconvenience caused. I'm afraid I'm not authorized to deal with refunds or exchanges over $100 without the approval of my manager. It's company policy.

C: It's ridiculous, that's what it is! You need to make some serious changes to your organization!

A: Thank you for your feedback, sir. I'll raise your concerns to my manager after this call.

C: Yes, you do that!

A: Now, could I get the names of the books you'd like to return?

C: Certainly. There are three books on marketing and one on … anger management.

A: Sorry, did you say, 'anger management'?

C: Yes, that's right.

A: Uh, I'm just going to put you on hold a minute if that's OK?

C: No, it isn't OK. I demand to …

Lesson 9.2 Listening, Exercise B

9.5 **P = Presenter D = Dawn**

P: I'm here today with Professor Dawn Jackson, from BLB University, who has just written a book, *Science Fact or Fiction?*, which focuses on common health myths related to the food industry. So Professor Jackson, can you give us an example of one of the myths you discuss in the book?

D: Well, possibly one of the most common myths is that we need to drink two liters of water every day.

P: Is that a myth? I definitely remember hearing that we should try to drink at least eight glasses of water a day to stay hydrated.

D: Well, yes, that's the claim but there isn't really any evidence to support it. We get plenty of water through food. Even drinks like coffee, which some people believe dehydrate you, are actually a good source of water. The bottom line is – trust your body. It will tell you when you're dehydrated.

P: So, where has this myth come from?

D: Well, I don't know the exact origins, but it's certainly useful for the bottled water industry, isn't it? They make billions of dollars a year.

P: Yes, it's a huge industry these days, isn't it? When I was a kid, no one drank bottled water.

D: Yes, the industry has grown rapidly with flavored water, vitamin drinks and even water that claims to be some kind of energy drink! All sorts of varieties.

P: Surely the added vitamins and minerals help?

D: No, not really. This is another huge myth created by creative advertising. A large number of people think taking vitamin C is a good way of fighting a cold, but there is no evidence this is the case. Actually, once you have a cold it will do very little to help you fight it. Vitamin C is good for you, but increasing your intake once you have an infection won't help fight it in the slightest.

P: So what should people do? How can they tell whether a claim is true or not?

D: Well, it really comes down to thinking critically about the things you read. Don't just take claims made in advertising at face value. If you're interested in a product, especially a health product, do a little research into the claim. Is there any scientific evidence to support it? Have there been multiple large-scale studies that consistently give the same results? Only then can you be confident that a claim is based on real evidence.

P: So we need to do a little homework?

D: Exactly!

P: OK, so we asked our listeners to send in their questions and one topic that kept coming up is yogurts. They're good for digestion, aren't they?

D: Well, depending on the type of yogurt – yes. Most yogurt sold in the US is described as 'live yogurt' because it contains living bacteria. The proper name for this type of bacteria is probiotics, but you've probably heard them described as 'friendly bacteria'. This is because they're widely thought to help your digestive system.

P: But wasn't a large yogurt company – I won't say who – actually taken to court over false claims linking yogurt to digestion?

D: Yes, that's true, but that was largely due to the wording they used in their ads. You just can't say something is 'scientifically proven' if you don't have enough evidence to support your claim. In fact, in Europe, companies actually have to get the approval of the European Food Safety Authority – the EFSA – before they're allowed to make health claims in their ads. In the US, they need approval by the Food and Drug Administration – the FDA. Applications are frequently rejected by the EFSA or FDA because the company simply doesn't have enough evidence to support their claim.

P: So I guess companies have to word their ads pretty carefully?

D: That's right. You can say things like 'may help to aid digestion', but you can't say 'clinically proven to help aid digestion' unless you back this up with evidence.

P: So another hot topic for our listeners is sugar. Is it really that bad for you?

D: I'm afraid so, yes. Overconsumption of 'free sugars' – those that have been added to things like sodas or chocolate – can lead to weight gain, which ultimately is linked to things like heart disease, cancer and diabetes. They're obviously really bad for your teeth, too.

P: But doesn't fruit contain a lot of sugar?

D: Uh, it does, but it also contains fiber which actually slows down the rate at which the body absorbs sugar. You'd have to eat *a lot* of fruit to get the same amount of sugar as you'd get from, say, a soda.

P: So I'm OK to keep drinking a smoothie every morning then?

D: Actually, no. When you blend fruit into a smoothie, the natural sugars are released – meaning you consume more sugar than you would by just eating a piece of fruit.

P: Really? But I always think of them as being healthy!

D: Ha ha! Just another example of creative advertising, I'm afraid.

UNIT 10

Lesson 10.1 Reading, Exercise B

10.1 **S = Sally P1 = Press 1 P2 = Press 2 P3 = Press 3**

S: Good morning. It is with a heavy heart that I announce the discontinuation of *Healthy Me* as a print publication. From our January issue onward, the magazine will be exclusively available in a digital format on all portable devices. I will now take questions from the press.

P1: James Patterson, *CBNR*. What motivated the shift away from print?

S: Well, sales have been falling for five years now. We've gone from a distribution of just over 500,000 copies a month to under 100,000. During the same period, downloads of the *Healthy Me* app have increased by almost 300%. In fact, yesterday saw the total number of registered users reach over one million. It's just clear from the numbers that the majority of our readers prefer to consume content online.

P2: Emily Davis, the *Evening Inquirer*. Will other publications from LMI Media make the same transition?

S: Uh, no, not yet anyway. However, I'm sure all magazine publishers will start to re-evaluate their options over the next five to ten years.

P3: Martin Webb, *CityTimes.com*. What does this trend mean for print media in general?

S: Well, I think that really depends on the type of publication. For example, despite the increased popularity of e-readers, people still seem to love physical copies of fiction titles. Students still seem to prefer printed textbooks over digital. However, for lifestyle magazines, like ours, which are predominantly directed toward a younger audience, it simply doesn't make financial sense to produce print media any longer. Fewer young people are buying physical media, and we have to recognize this if we're to continue publishing our magazine. Thank you.

Lesson 10.1 Listening, Exercise C

10.2 **P = Presenter E = Emily**

P: Fake news is a phrase and a concept that didn't even really exist a few years ago, but today it's one of the biggest buzzwords in the media. To discuss why fake news has become so prevalent and what, if anything, can be done about it, I have journalist Emily Woolf with me here today. So, Emily, what exactly is fake news?

E: Essentially, it is news that is not true. Some of it is clearly written as a joke and is simply there to amuse people, but a lot of it is written in a way so as to trick the reader. The writer wants you to believe that it is genuine news.

P: So, how new is the concept of fake news?

E: Well, it's not new at all, really. There has always been fake news, but in the past it was less common, largely because there was no money to be made from it. All of a newspaper's income was made from advertising and no company wanted to advertise alongside fake news articles because it wasn't good for their reputation. You may have found an occasional fake story in a tabloid because they didn't always have such high standards, but you certainly wouldn't have found any in the high-end newspapers.

P: So, what's changed?

E: In a word, the internet. The internet and social media have been massive game changers. It's so much easier for people to share stories and they don't always check that they're true before they do so.

P: But surely, advertisers still want to be associated with good quality content?

E: To a certain extent, yes, but advertising on the internet is based on search engines knowing what you like to look at and then showing you ads that you want to click on, so the association with the content has been lost a little, I think. These days, advertisements and headlines appear together on your news feed and are tailored to your personal tastes or behaviors online, usually showing you more of the same thing. The problem is it can be difficult to tell what the source of a headline is, so it may look similar to genuine news providers, and when you click through it , it's very difficult to tell if the website is genuine or not.

P: That's true. I frequently click on links to websites just based on the headline and the websites look very professional once you get there.

E: They are, and it can be difficult to tell if the news is fake or real. We're no longer so sure which sources to trust. Traditionally, print newspapers have been held to a much higher standard. In other words, unlike bloggers and people writing on social media, large newspapers can't just lie or make things up. I think we used to have more faith in sources like CNN, but now people don't know who to trust. In the past, we could be fairly certain information from those sources was real. We could also tell fairly easily which articles were factual and which ones contained opinions that could be biased or subjective.

P: So, you think some traditional media outlets could be biased or subjective?

E: Yes. Definitely! Let me rephrase that, personal opinion always comes into journalism so there will inevitably be articles that reflect the views of the writer. In the past, it was much clearer that these were simply opinions. Now, some 'opinions' are presented as 'facts'.

P: This is obviously a huge problem.

E: It is. The problem is that people tend to believe a lot of the things they read. Despite the ease of searching on the internet, people don't tend to check the facts in a story on various other sites or from different sources. They are especially likely to believe stories about serious issues.

P: So if someone writes an article, for example, claiming that climate change is a myth, people will usually believe it.

E: Unfortunately, yes. That's a good example actually. Pretty much all scientists agree that climate change is real and there's a lot of evidence to support it. To be more precise, the only real debate is how quickly it is happening and how bad the effects will be. It's very worrying, and dangerous, that several people might read one article and go away with the conclusion that it isn't happening.

P: So, what can be done about fake news? Who should be responsible for controlling it?

E: Governments need to take a much stronger stance. Anyone writing news should be held accountable to the same standards as a journalist. Editors of newspapers were always held responsible for the content of the newspaper whereas website owners aren't necessarily. In other words, the owners of these sites need to be held responsible for the content of their site.

P: The problem there, is that people read websites from all around the world and there might not be the same rules in one country as another.

E: That's true. One other thing that would be useful is encouraging people, students especially, to think critically. Who wrote the text? What is the source? Why was it written? I know some schools are now training students to spot fake news and I think that could really help. In a recent study 75% of students, excuse me 79%, were unable to accurately identify fake news stories.

P: Wow! That's shocking. Critical thinking is clearly a skill people need to learn at a young age. OK, let's see how easy it is to spot fake news. Here are some headlines. Are they real or fake?

Lesson 10.2 Listening, Exercise A

10.5 **P = Presenter**

P: No doubt many of you have seen videos and posts that have gone viral, such as the mannequin challenge, the running man challenge or silly challenges like recreating the 'Harlem Shake' video. When these things start trending, or get a popular hashtag, they can really take off. Some organizations have been smart enough to realize that this meme concept can be used to help charities.

Many of you have no doubt also heard of Movember and the Ice Bucket Challenge, both of which started off small, but grew to capture the world's attention. The Movember event was conceived in Australia by two friends – Travis Garone and Luke Slattery – who were joking about reviving old trends. Inspired by a friend's mother who was fundraising for breast cancer, they decided to use the idea for a good cause – to raise money for prostate cancer and other men's health issues. In its first year, the event made no money and only had 30 participants. By 2014, it had exploded and garnered 1.2 million mentions on social media, with participants in over 20 countries.

Movember gradually built success over a sustained period of time, but the Ice Bucket Challenge took off much more quickly and, arguably, had a larger overall reach. In 2014, Facebook, Twitter and Instagram were flooded with people challenging each other to throw a bucket of iced water over their head to raise awareness of ALS – a disease that affects nerve cells in the brain. The campaign got over two billion online mentions that year and in the first three months, 15 million videos of willing victims were shared on Facebook. These were viewed 10 billion times by 440 million people in countries all over the globe, which in turn led to a significant increase in donations to charity groups like the ALS Foundation. For example, in 2013 ALS's best week saw them raise $25,000, yet after the campaign it raised $2.4 million dollars in one week.

So, what made these campaigns go viral? Well, research from Sander van der Linden, a psychology professor from the University of Cambridge, tells us that watching an act of kindness performed by a peer makes people want to behave in a similar manner. These effective campaigns also help us to better understand the condition these people are suffering from. They encourage people to act and inspire positive reactions from people.

So, how can we use this research to influence the content we create? In order to create good viral content, you need to understand your target audience. In other words, you need to know who you are trying to reach and how. Campaigns only go viral if they speak to people on a personal level, so you need to create an image that represents the demographic, that is the age and gender of the people you want to reach. For example, if you want to target women aged between 18–24, then it's probably a good idea to try and incorporate Pinterest into your campaign since the majority of the platform's users fit this demographic.

Second, you need to create content that has high levels of engagement. Most social media platforms rank content using incredibly complex algorithms. If you don't create engaging content, it will receive a low ranking and is far less likely to be shared as a result. Short videos typically go viral if they are shocking, memorable or funny because viral marketing is about emotions. People will share content that makes them react emotionally and this is the key to rapid growth. Using a hook that makes people happy or makes them laugh will make the content go viral.

So, once you have a good campaign together, how do you spread the word? One efficient way to promote your campaign is to use social media influencers. Social media influencers have the ability to give brands a reach they wouldn't normally get. We've all seen, and been jealous of, people paid to travel the world and share their experiences online. Most of these are social media influencers who are usually paid to promote brands.

Capturing contact information is also vital because, although it is fairly easy to create a viral success, it is phenomenally difficult to maintain this success long-term. Charities, for example, need long-term regular donations, rather than just one great year. Finding a way to encourage people to give you their email address will allow you to build a relationship long-term and gain regular payments from them. One way to get people to hand over their email address is to offer something for free. The word 'free' is a great way to get people engaged and is one of the best hooks you can utilize. I'm sure a lot of you are here today because the talk is free and we have free coffee!

Finally, some kind of competitive challenge is always fun. This challenge could be fun or silly, but ideally a combination of both, since this tends to be what engages people the most. It also needs to create an emotional reaction to the charity being supported. In just a few seconds, you have taken people on an emotional rollercoaster and gone viral.

Notes

Macmillan Education Limited
4 Crinan Street
London N1 9XW

Companies and representatives throughout the world

American Language Hub Level 4B Student's Book ISBN 978-1-380-04741-0
American Language Hub Level 4B Student's Book with Student's App
ISBN 978-1-380-04735-9

Written by Louis Rogers

First published 2020

Designed by emc design ltd
Illustrated by Daniel Limón (Beehive illustration) pp 75, 88, 89, 90, XVIII
Cover design by Restless
Cover photograph by plainpicture/Westend61/Uwe Umstätter
Picture research by Emily Taylor

Authentic video footage supplied by BBC Studios Distribution Limited
Café Hub videos produced by Sharp Focus

The authors and publishers would like to thank the following for permission to reproduce their photographs:

Alamy/Aldamisa Entertainment pp86–87, Fotorince p65, Nino Marcutti pp76–77; **E+** p115; **Getty Images** AFP/STR p104(tr), Anadolu Agency p70(br), Lorraine Boogich p78(Christina), Caiaimage/Paul Viant p106(br), Matt Cardy p80, Guido Cavallini pXXII, Chinaface p74, David Colbert/EyeEm p114(br), Shaun Curry p113, Peter Dazeley p92, Jan Diepeveen/EyeEm p114(tr), Digital Vision p78(Chris), Alessandro Di Ciommo/NurPhoto p67, Eternalcreative pXIX, EyeEm pp102, XXIV, Graiki pp82–83(background), Mike Harrington p73, Hero Images pp93, 106(bl), Ralf Hettler p89(tr), Hill Street Studios p81, Image Source pp70–71(background), iStockphoto pp66–67(background), 89(br), Juanmonino p116(bl), Justin Lewis p85, Matt84 p89(cr), Nathalie Michel p97, Momo productions pp78(Hayley), 110, Nikada p94(tr), Leo Patrizi p111, Michelle Patrick/EyeEm pp118–119, Witthaya Prasongsin p82(tr), Tim Robberts p78(Kelly), RooM RF p98, Selimaksan p116(tr), Claudio Sericano/EyeEm pp106–107(background), Kirstin Sinclair p104(br), Linda Steward p86(l), Sturti p62, Taxi p78(Nick), Julie Toy p61, Klaus Vedfelt p118, Claudio Villa p117, Dong Wenjie p112, Westend61 pp78(Sam), 101, Brent Winebrenner p109, WireImage p104(tl), Alex Wong p104(tm), Jacobo Zanella pp94–95

Commissioned photographs by Sharp Focus pp71, 83, 95, 107, 119

The author and publishers are grateful for permission to reprint the following copyright material: Extract from '2 Most Viral Social Media Campaigns of this Decade so far!' by Salman Aslam. © 2009–2019 Omnicore Agency. All rights reserved. Reprinted with permission of Omnicore Agency, pp116–117.

Printed and bound in Brazil

2025

13